I0798537

Open the Gates

Poems for Young Readers

Also by Dabney Stuart

Poetry

The Diving Bell (1966)
A Particular Place (1969)
The Other Hand (1974)
Round and Round: A Triptych (1977)
Rockbridge Poems (1981)
Common Ground (1982)
Don't Look Back (1987)
Narcissus Dreaming (1990)
Light Years: New and Selected Poems (1994)
Second Sight: Poems for Paintings by Carroll Cloar (1996)
Long Gone (1996)
Settlers (1999)
The Man Who Loves Cézanne (2003)
Family Preserve (2005)
Tables (2009)

Fiction

Sweet Lucy Wine (1991)
The Way to Cobbs Creek (1997)
No Visible Means of Support (2001)

For Children

Friends of Yours, Friends of Mind (1974)

Criticism

Nabokov: The Dimensions of Parody (1978)

Also by Susan E. Elliott

Fiction

Ophelia's Ghost (2008)

Non-Fiction

Making the Most of WriteItNow 4 (2010)
Remembering the Parables (2010)

Illustrations

Spilled Milk: Haiku Destinies (2010)

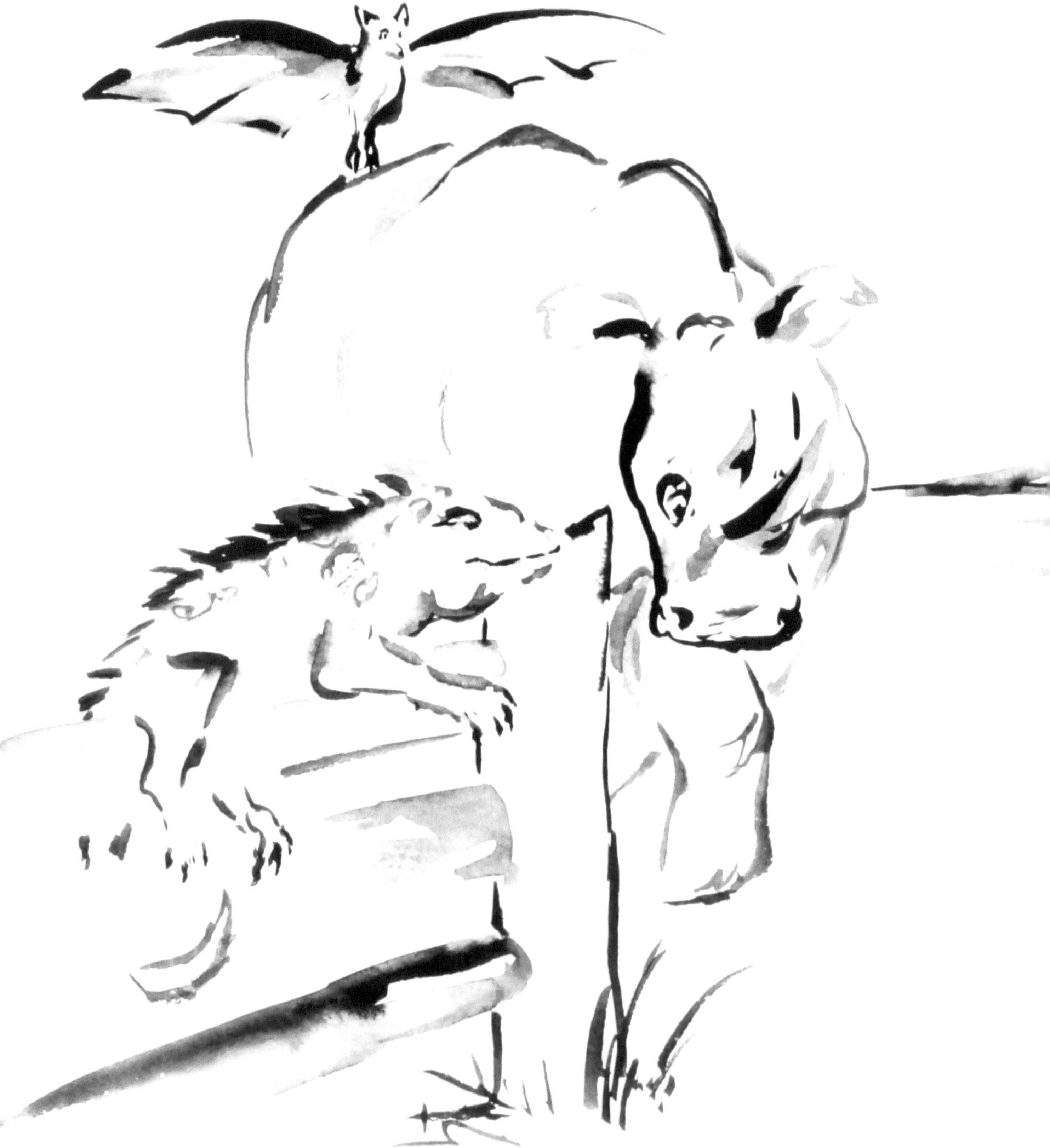

Open the Gates

Poems for Young Readers

by Dabney Stuart

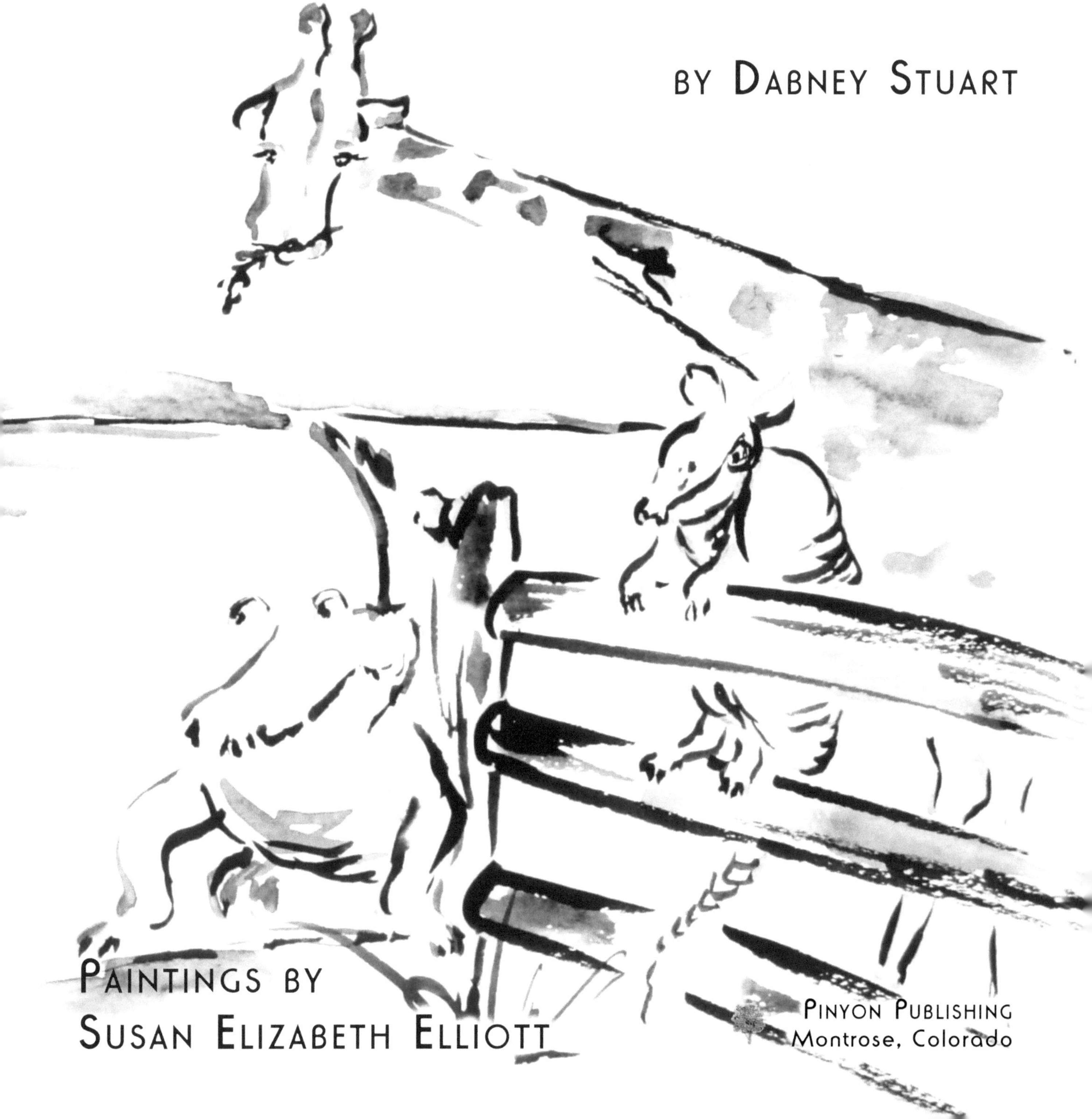

Paintings by
Susan Elizabeth Elliott

Pinyon Publishing
Montrose, Colorado

Copyright © 2010 by Walker Dabney Stuart TTE, Walker Dabney Stuart Trust u/a/d November 2001

All rights reserved. Except as permitted under the U.S. Copyright Act of 1976, no part of this publication may be reproduced, distributed, or transmitted in any form or by any means, or stored in a database or retrieval system, without the prior written permission of the publisher, except for brief quotations in articles, books, and reviews.

Paintings copyright © 2010 by Susan E. Elliott
Photograph of Dabney Stuart copyright © 2010 by Sandra Stuart
Photograph of Susan Elliott copyright © 2010 by Bill Elliott

A few of these poems, in different forms, previously appeared in Mr. Stuart's volume, "Friends of Yours, Friends of Mine."

First Edition: 2010

Pinyon Publishing
23847 V66 Trail, Montrose, CO 81403
www.pinyon-publishing.com

Library of Congress Control Number: 2010930752
ISBN: 978-0-9821561-6-2

For

Billie & Elliot

and

Jamaica

And for Jack & Sam

Contents

One

Two

Three

Four

Five

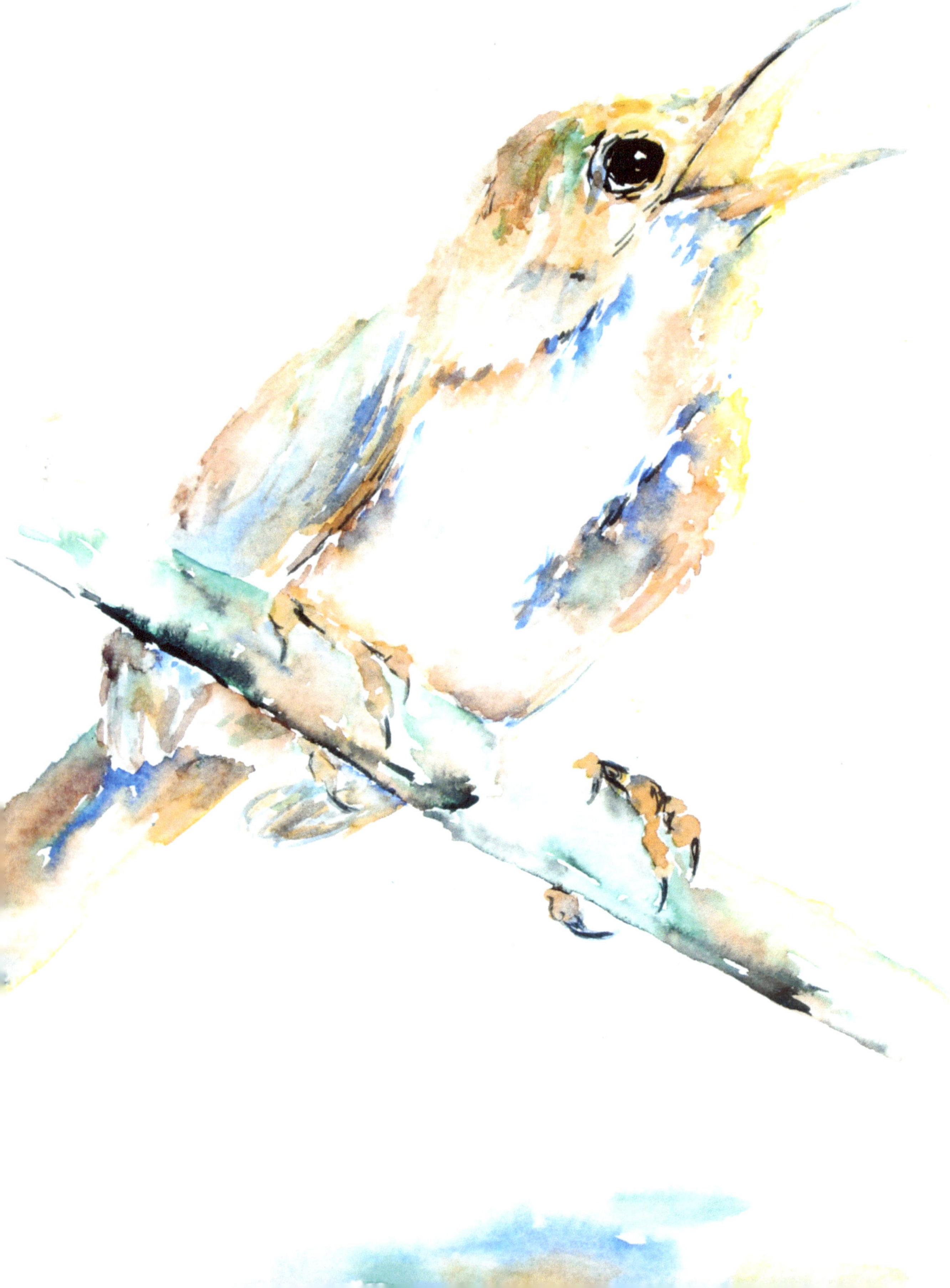

OPEN THE GATES...

The sun said, "Open the gates
        Open the gates!
I have been down here in the dark
        too long.

Any self-respecting sun hates
        this infernal waiting.
Let me up to the light, as a lark
        to song."

So the gates opened, or the sun
        opened the gates,
and rose up and was light and gave light
        everywhere

in sight and out of sight,
        on plates
at tables and through cracks in doors,
        in blue air

and green, on wrens and lemon trees
        and peppers hanging
by their fingers, and you and me
        out here

where the gates open to...

One

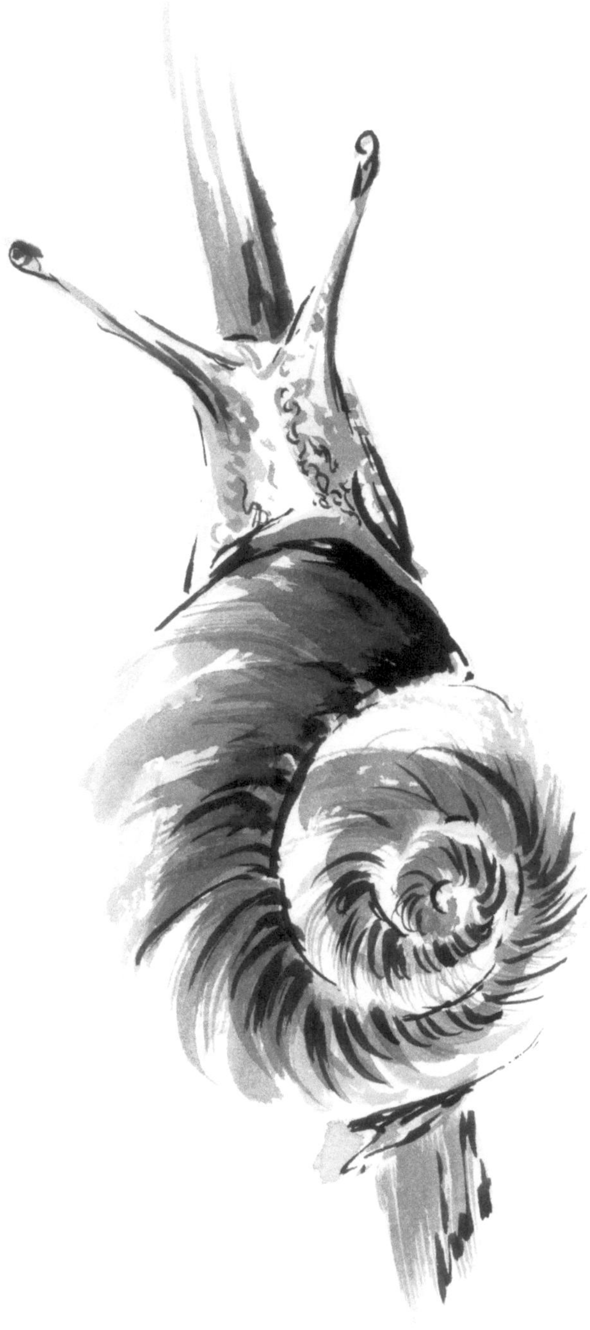

SANDBOX CREATURES

Get your buckets
  and shovels
together, and your bare feet
  on.

The sand's awake
  and waiting,
and just damp enough
  for you

to dig up and plant
  all
the upside-down buckets-
  full,

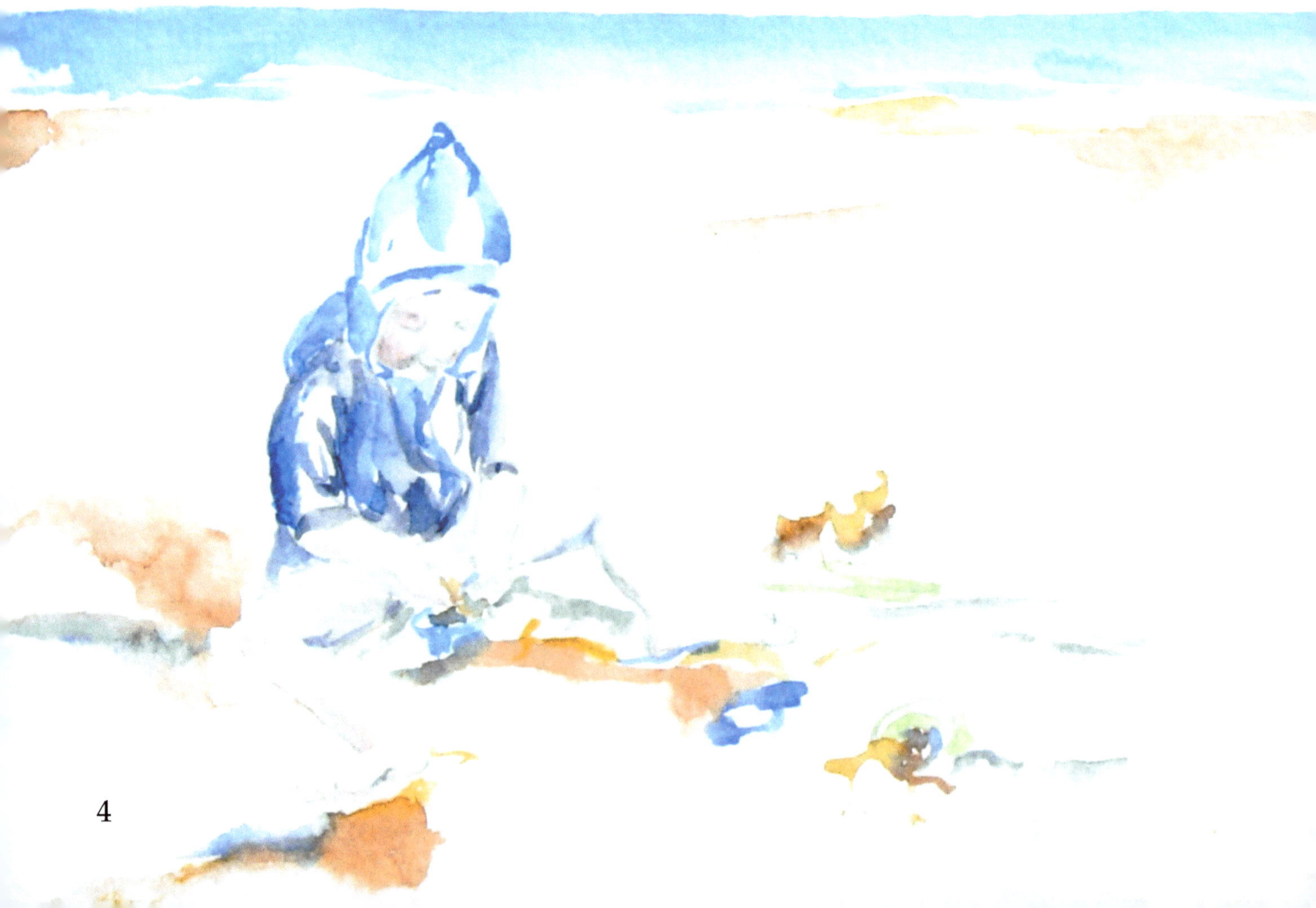

those bumpy rows
of bottoms-up
cones
with their tips

sliced off. Are they new
animals,
maybe, or footprints
made

from inside the ground
by a trapped
creature with its head
pointed

toward the center
of the earth?
How lightly, then,
it walks

on your fair
morning
and the planet's grains of
sand.

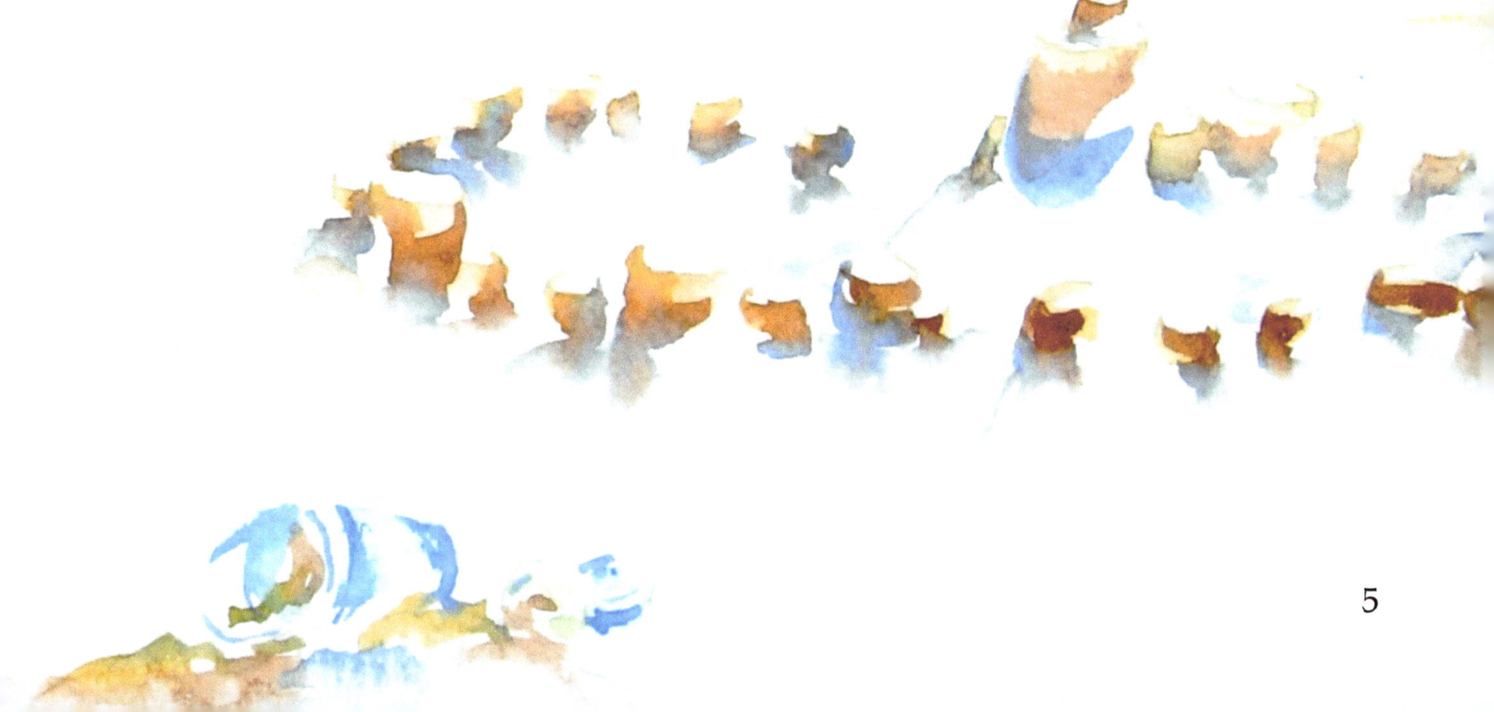

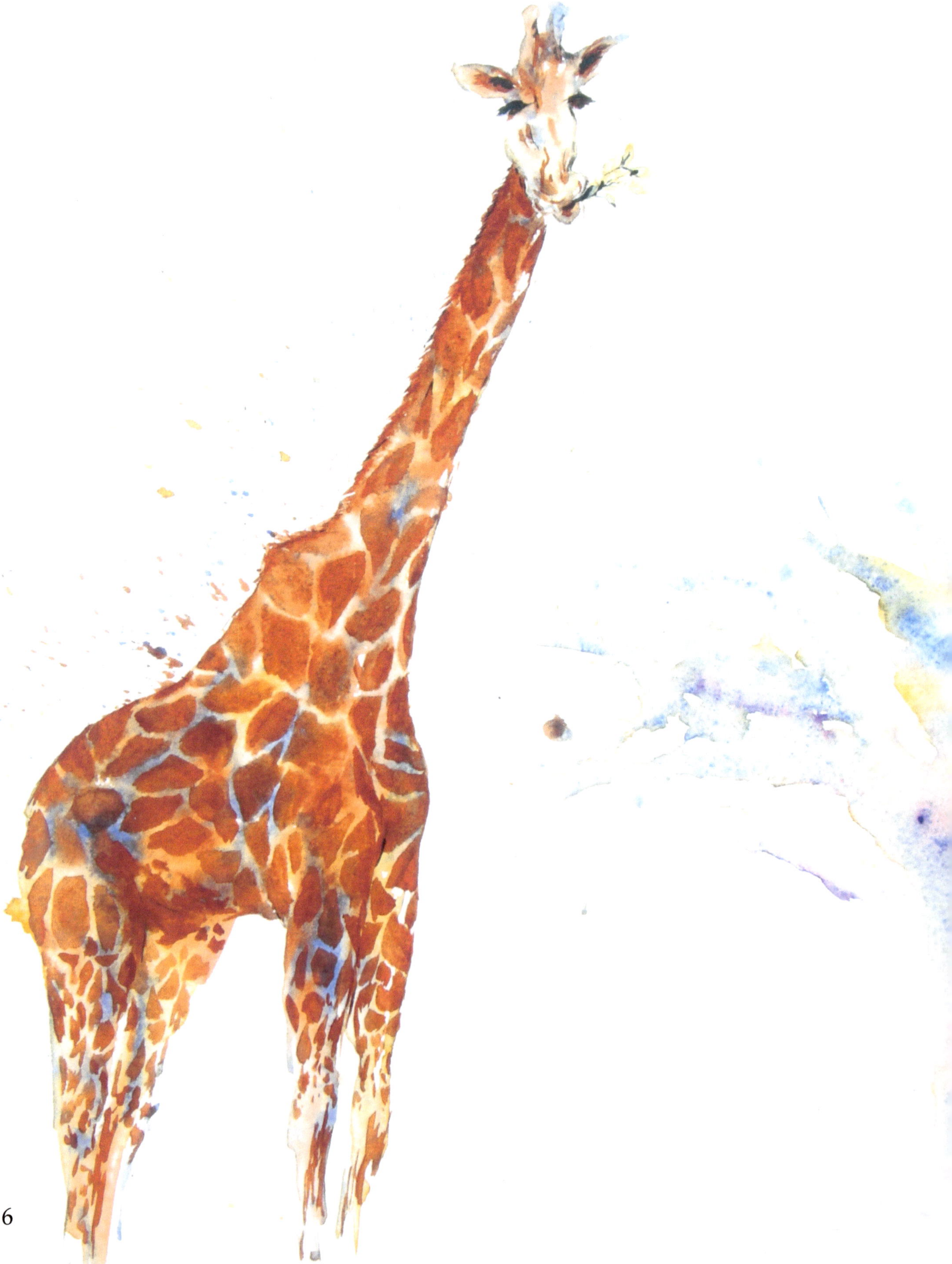

GIRAFFE

She sees
a world of sky and trees.

The leaves hang down around her
head and neck,

a shower
for her to mosey in, and hunt and pick

and munch.
Her breakfast, lunch,

and dinner take all day.
She eats away

the hours up there, moving from one
abundance

to another in the dappling sun.
Light's dance

on her skin's soft patchwork puzzle
is another dazzle.

She hardly sleeps,
at all, but when she does she keeps

her head up there in her weave
of sky and leaves.

BUMBLEBEES

Do bumblebees fumble—
    or even bumble?
They seem much too graceful
    and quick
for that, going back
    and forth from flower
to flowerful.

Do bumblebees mumble?
    not being clear
or precise,
    always saying to the other mumblebees,
Would you repeat that, please?

Do bumblebees tumble?
    rolling head over stinger,
not pausing to linger
    long in a cuplet of petals,
but spinning in air
    like miniature windmills?

Whatever we say about
        mum fum
stumblebees
        one thing's for sure—

a bumblebee's
        HUM ble.

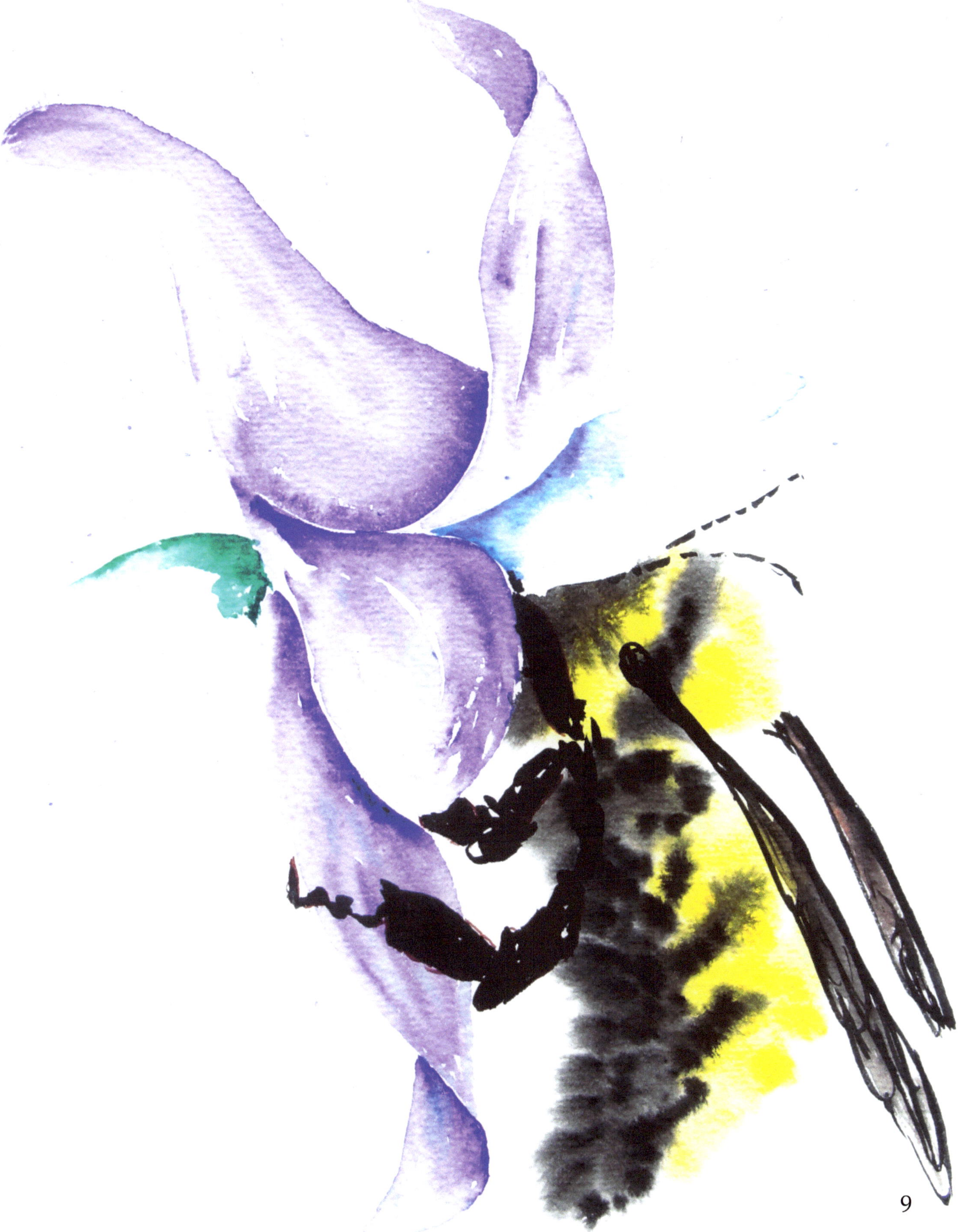

ARMADILLO

The armadillo's
a tricky fellow.
When he tries to run
he seems to wallow
in all that armor,
so you think he'd be slow.

But he's not! He's quick!
Ask any insect
who may still be around
after his sharp claws
do their speedy surround.
Another surprise
that some armadillos
keep under wraps
inside all that armor
is a life-saving hollow.
Throw one in the river:
he'll suck in some air
and not sink, but rise,
like a bell-singing buoy,
and float out of there.

With talents like these
the old armadillo
might do other things
nobody supposes.
Perhaps in his burrow
preparing for bed
he pulls his legs in
to his tired little body
and sleeps in his own pillow.

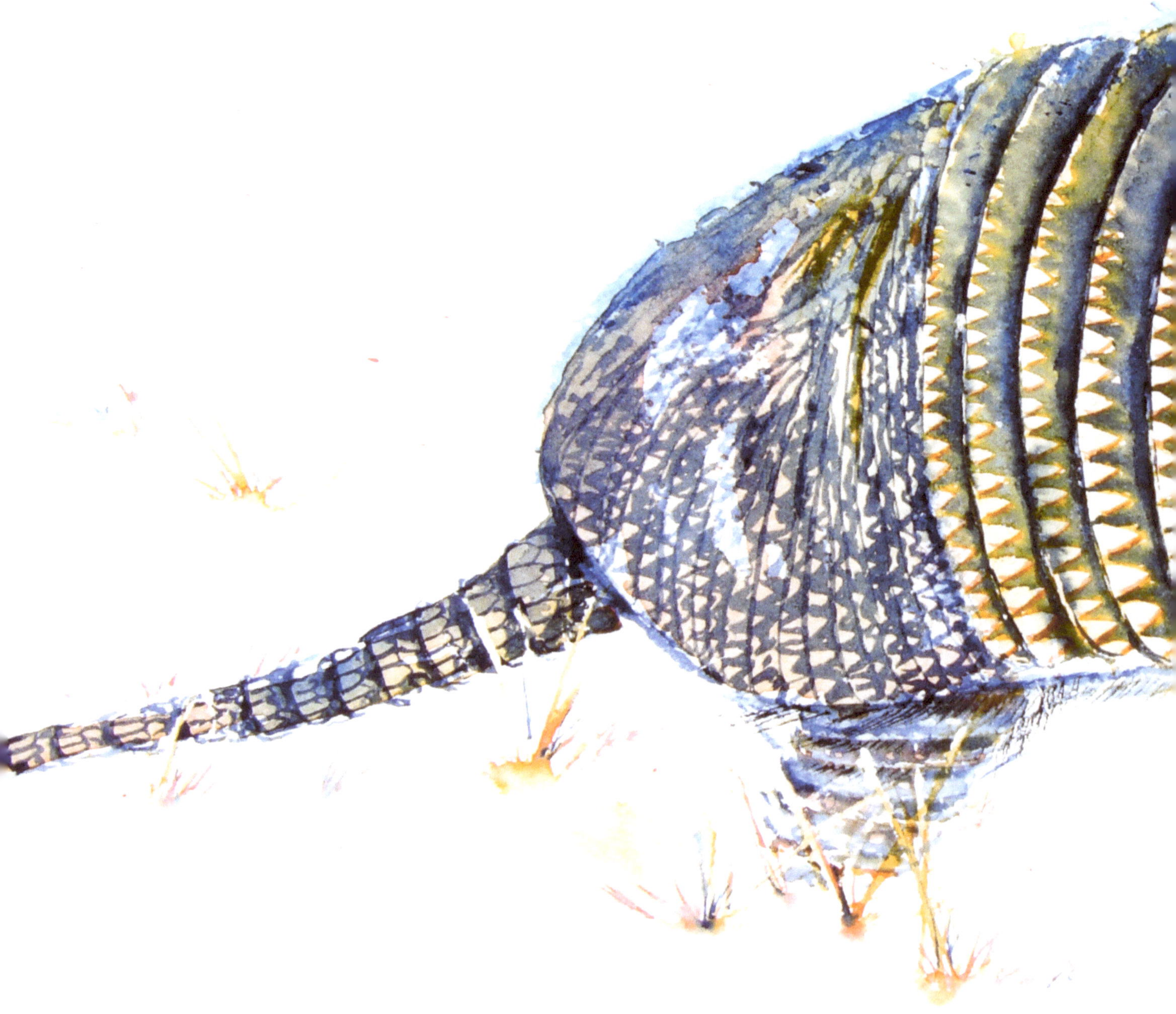

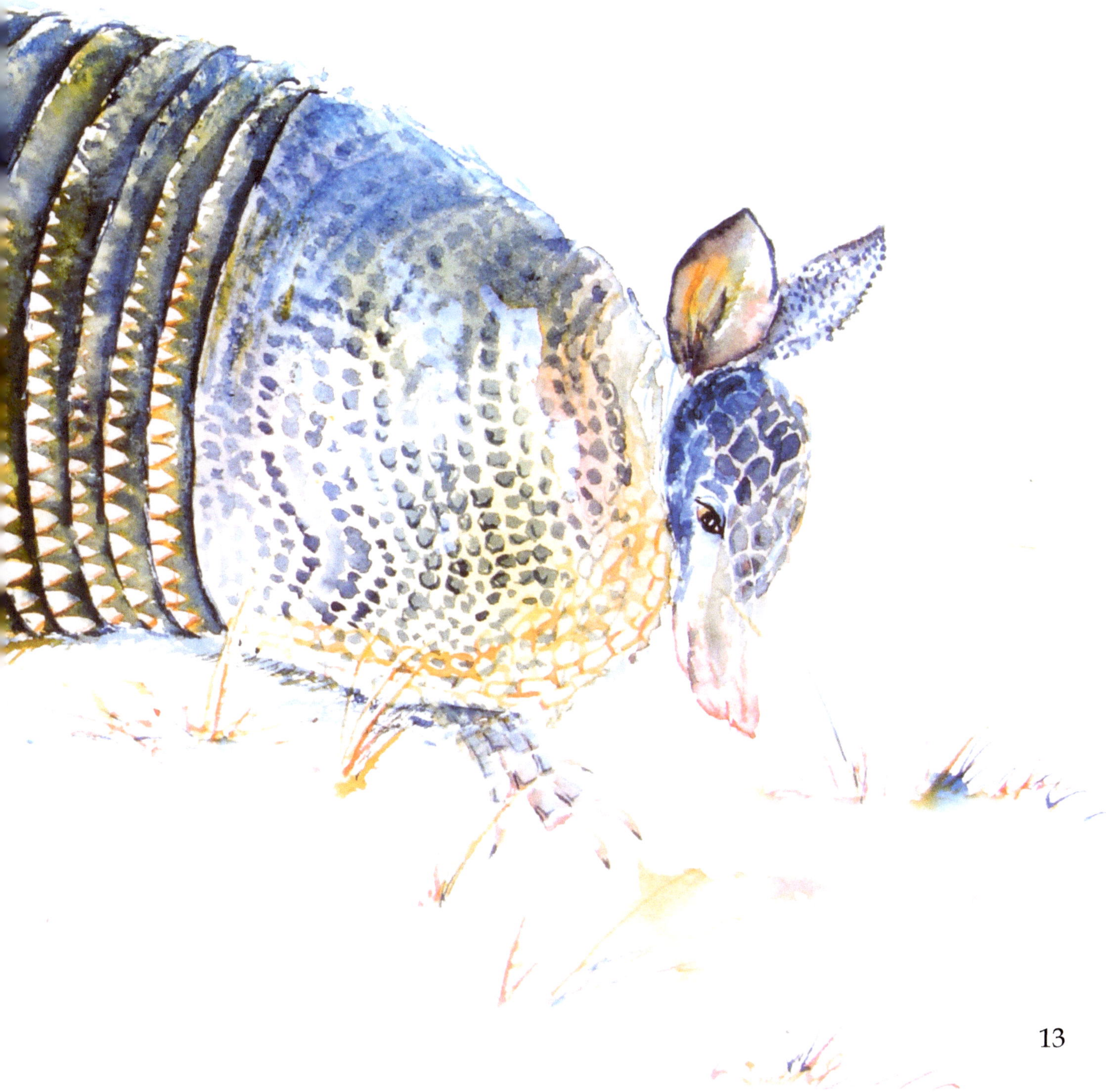

HUMMINGBIRD

The hummingbird's wings
are dainty things
which she keeps transparently trim;
they take her with ease
across the seas
and she doesn't have to swim.

This is one guest
to whom you say "Yes"
when she has to eat and fly;
she can fill up
from a tiny cup
before you can wink your eye.

When the sun rises
she's full of surprises,
her colors are dazzling and rare;
her red and green
are the brightest we've seen
from Texas to Delaware.

But you've got to look fast
or she'll zoom right past
and you'll never know she was there;
don't search for her nest
or where she might rest
because she's at home in the air.

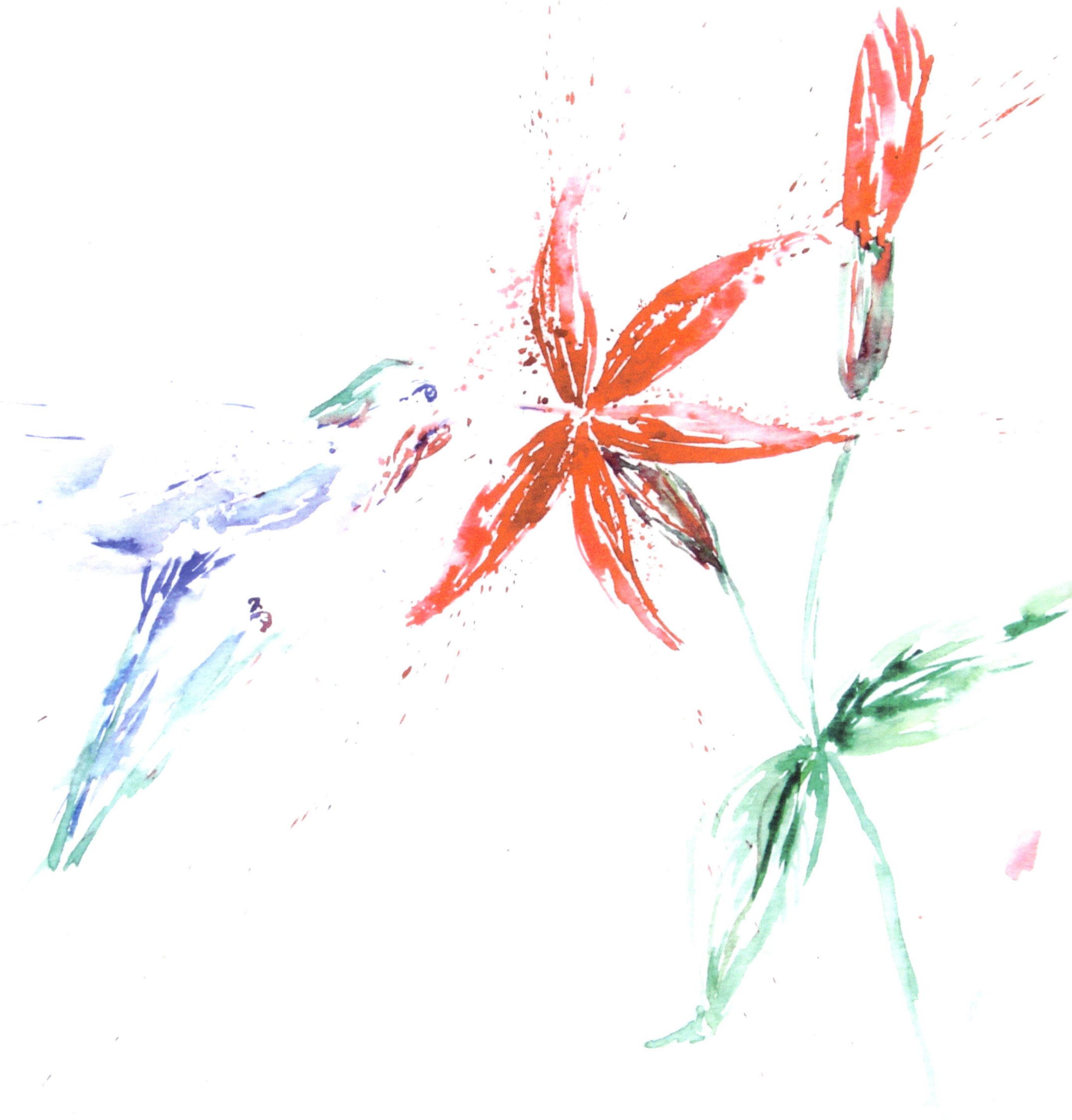

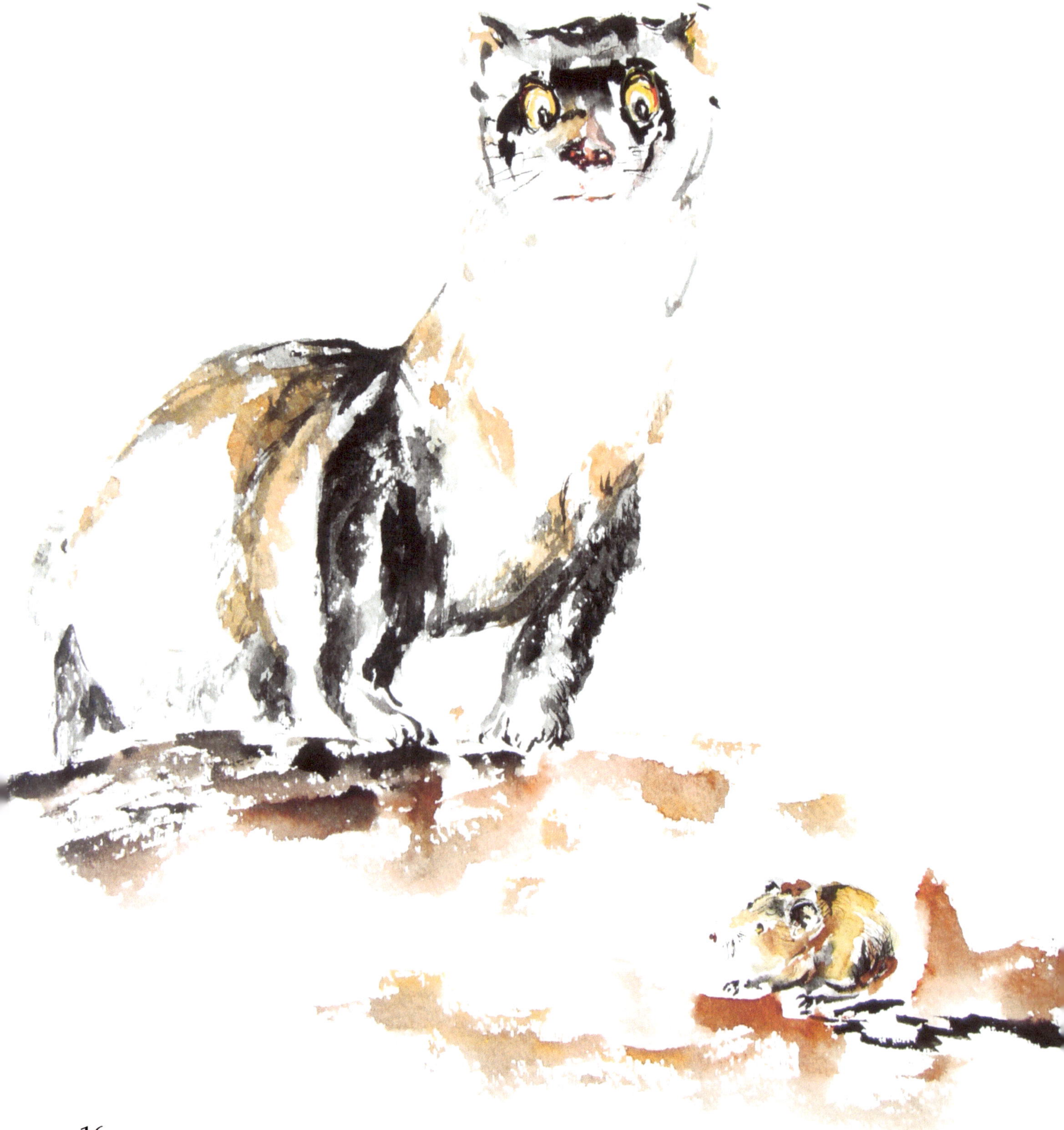

VOLES AND FERRETS

Voles and ferrets
  don't live in turrets,
or gather in groups
  for afternoon hoops,
or twirl their mustaches,
  or practice kersplashes
in rivers and pools.

When they're not in the zoo,
  what do they do?

They sharpen their tools
  for digging and eating
and flashing down holes
  and scooting
                    and rooting
around, and leaving no traces
  for me and for you
of how they get to
  their underground places.

IMPALA

The impala's horns
are shaped like a lyre,
curving in and away,
though there're no strings
for sweet fingers to play,
to make music ring
through the echoing air.
The veldt is forlorn
at the absence of song
from the impala's horns.

But he makes up for this
as he glides over the grasses,
by the way each horn spirals
from forehead to tip,
two corkscrews that ruffle
the whispering air.
It's a quieter song
than one plucked from a lyre.
If you listen with care
as the impala passes
it touches your ear
like the gentlest of kisses.

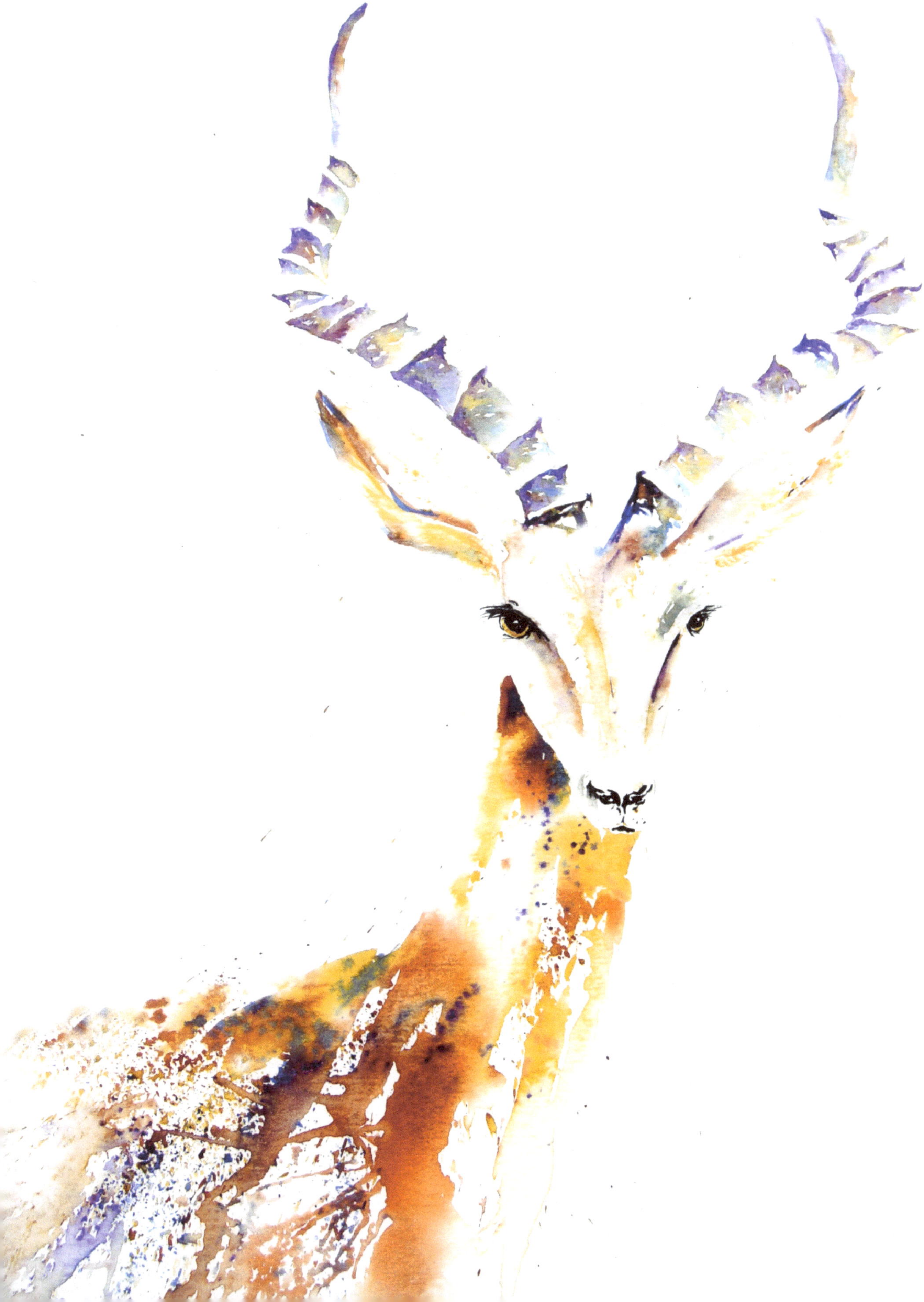

RHINOCEROS

When other animals panic
and run, or take flight,
in the face of danger,
the rhino turns.

When the scent of hunters rides
on the wind, or the sound
of their coming drifts there,
the rhino waits.

When the hunters set up
their camp and begin
to circle, their rifles ready,
the rhino charges.

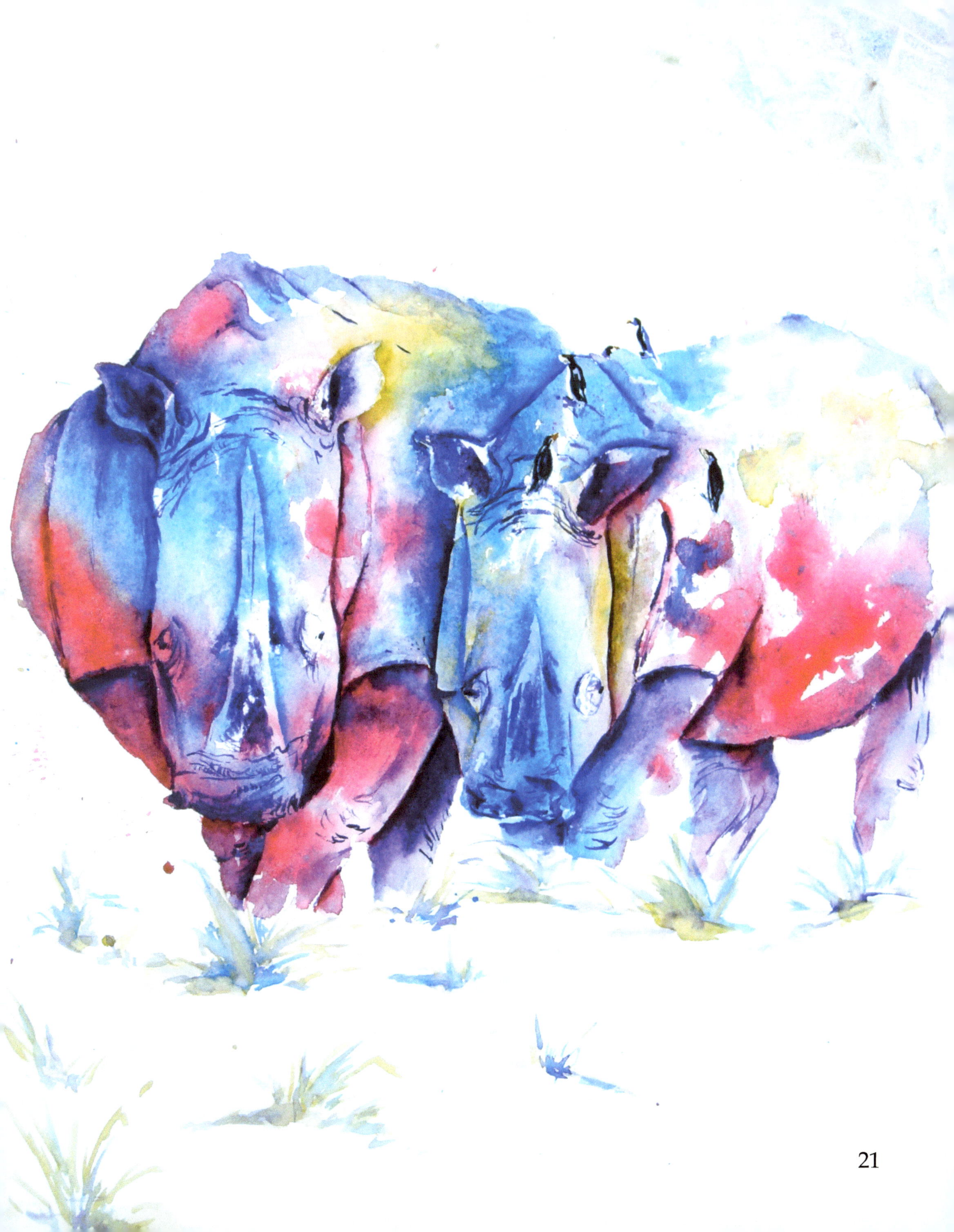

Two

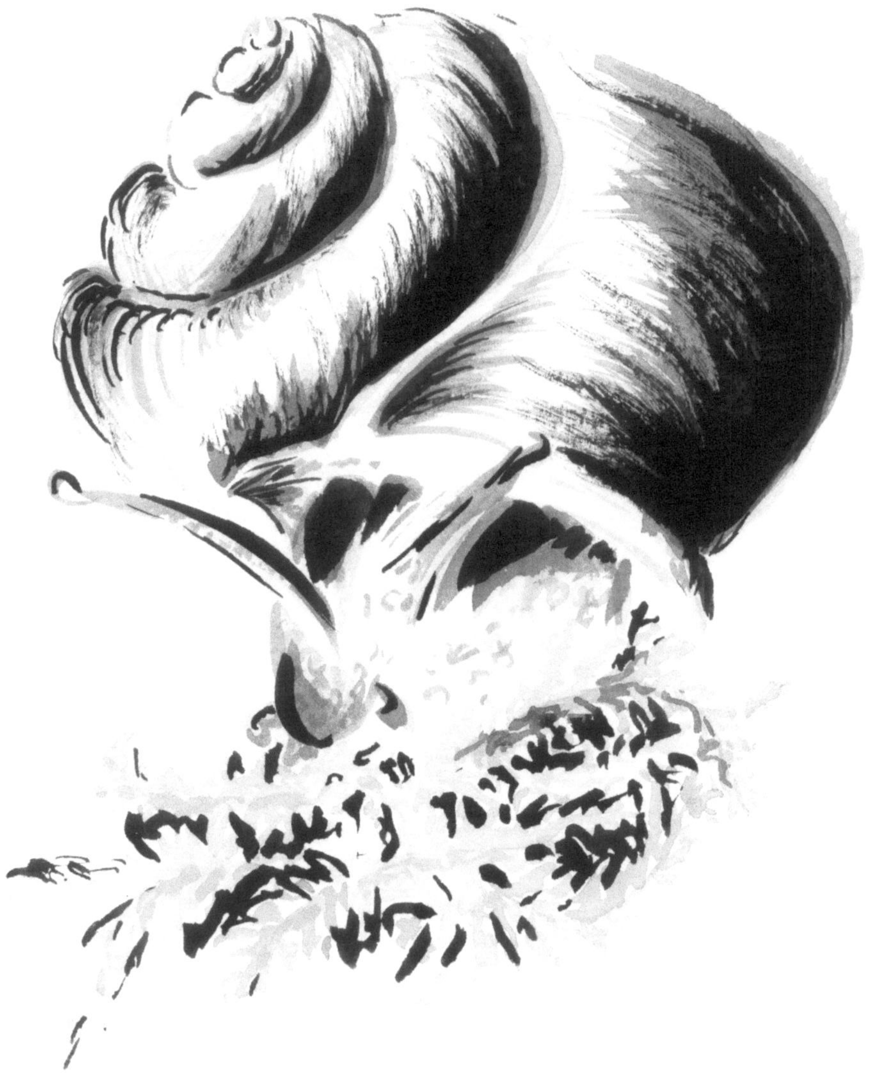

DOVE

When all the earth was covered
with water, and Noah wondered
if he'd see land again,
he released a dove in the air
twice, and the second time
the faithful bird returned
and laid an olive twig in his hand.
We know the flood receded
and Noah let down the plank
for all the animals to walk
on the solid ground they needed.

But while the dove was gone
those two weeks from the ark
somehow she kept from falling.
When all the earth was water
there was no roof or park
for her to perch on and rest.
In her unbroken flying
there was no place to nest.
Did she float some on the sea
or spend all her time in the air?
What did she find to eat?
Since she was just half a pair
she cooed to the empty sky,
her song unwinding and sweet
hoping for a reply.

If you want to learn about love
listen to the dove in the morning
call soft in her throat, and low,
for the memories that keep returning,
for the answers we'll never know.

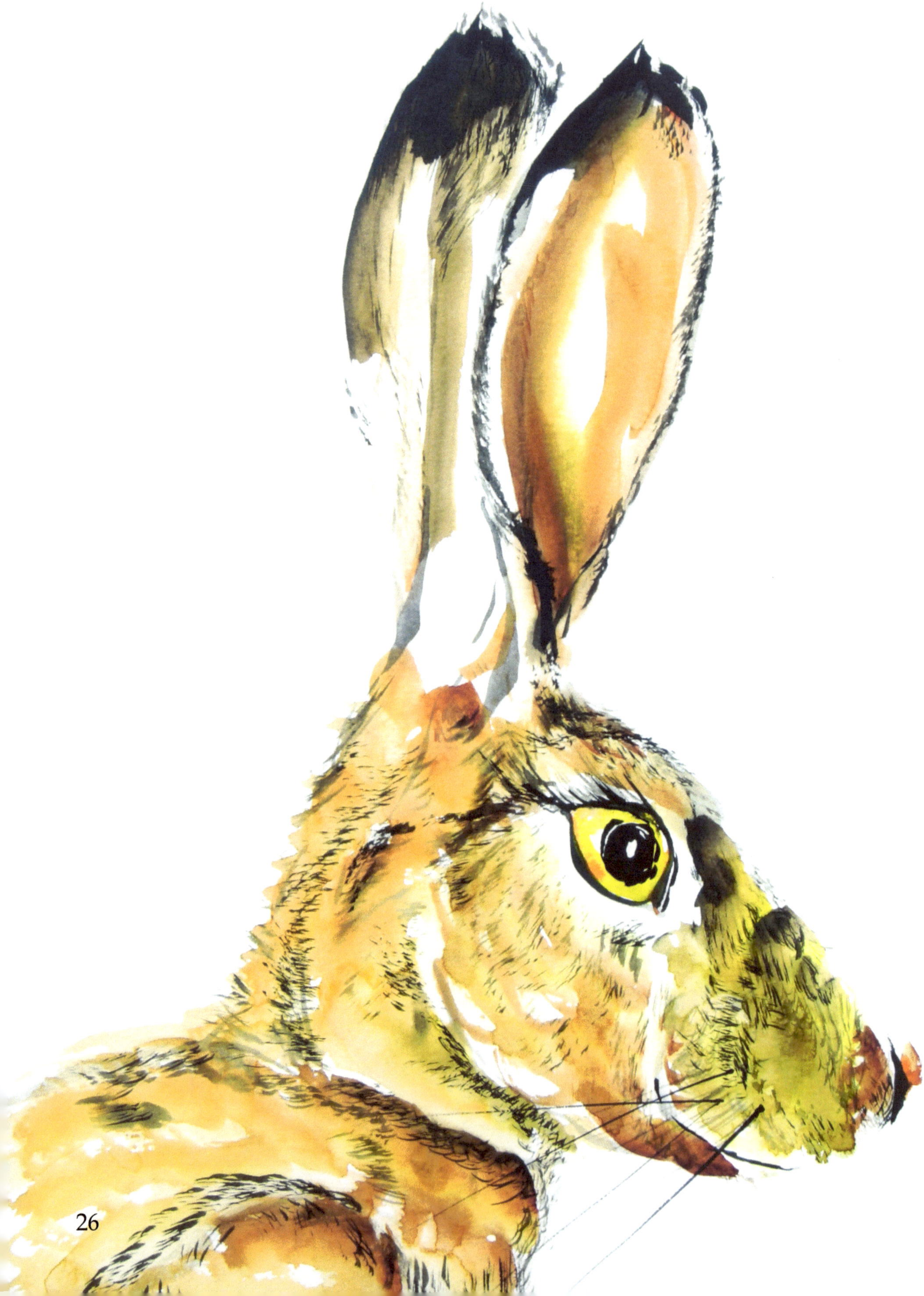

JACKRABBIT

He leaps high in the air.
He can stop on a dime.
Why should anyone care
if he's never on time?

He has legs full of vim;
he has ears to the sky.
Suppose he could flap them.
Suppose he could fly!

QUAIL

You've all seen the quail
cross the road
with her brood
pearled out behind her.
They don't quite sail
but they move
in a groove,
and they mind her!

It beats all the odds
how they stay
in their places
from one end to the other.
Their little foot pads
mark the dust
and get mussed
in the trail of their mother.

To march so exactly
whatever
the weather
must require careful training.
Yet how matter-of-factly
they define
their design,
and no one's complaining.

Though we don't have a clue
what new shape
they will take
when they stop single-filing,
whatever they do
when they slip
out of sight couldn't be as beguiling.

A BIRD, BUT WHO?

Who draws a circle in the sky,
Always keeps his feathers dry,
And likes to think he's quite a spy?

Who looks for animals on the ground,
Swoops upon them without a sound,
Flies to the nest, which is somewhere around?

Who's called the ugliest alive,
Although he makes a beautiful dive
Four times a day, and sometimes five?

Who wishes he had a handsome beak,
Well-oiled knees that never creak,
A tenor voice that doesn't squeak?

Who gets lonesome up in the blue,
Wants a change in life, something new,
Like a loyal friend—perhaps even you?
        The turkey buzzard, that's who.

NEWTS

There are scads of newts all over the globe,
from Maracaibo to Lagos, From Ghent to Latrobe,
doing their moseys and darts and meanders—
preparing, in time, to be salamanders.

There are tritons and smoothies and spotties galore
inhabiting niches in Minsk and Indore,
skittering and sliding and cavorting and such—
growing up, and liking it all very much.

But none are as neat as the red newt, who's bred
two or three years on the land, where he's red:
he then switches to water, where he turns a dull green
with red spots to remind him of who he has been.

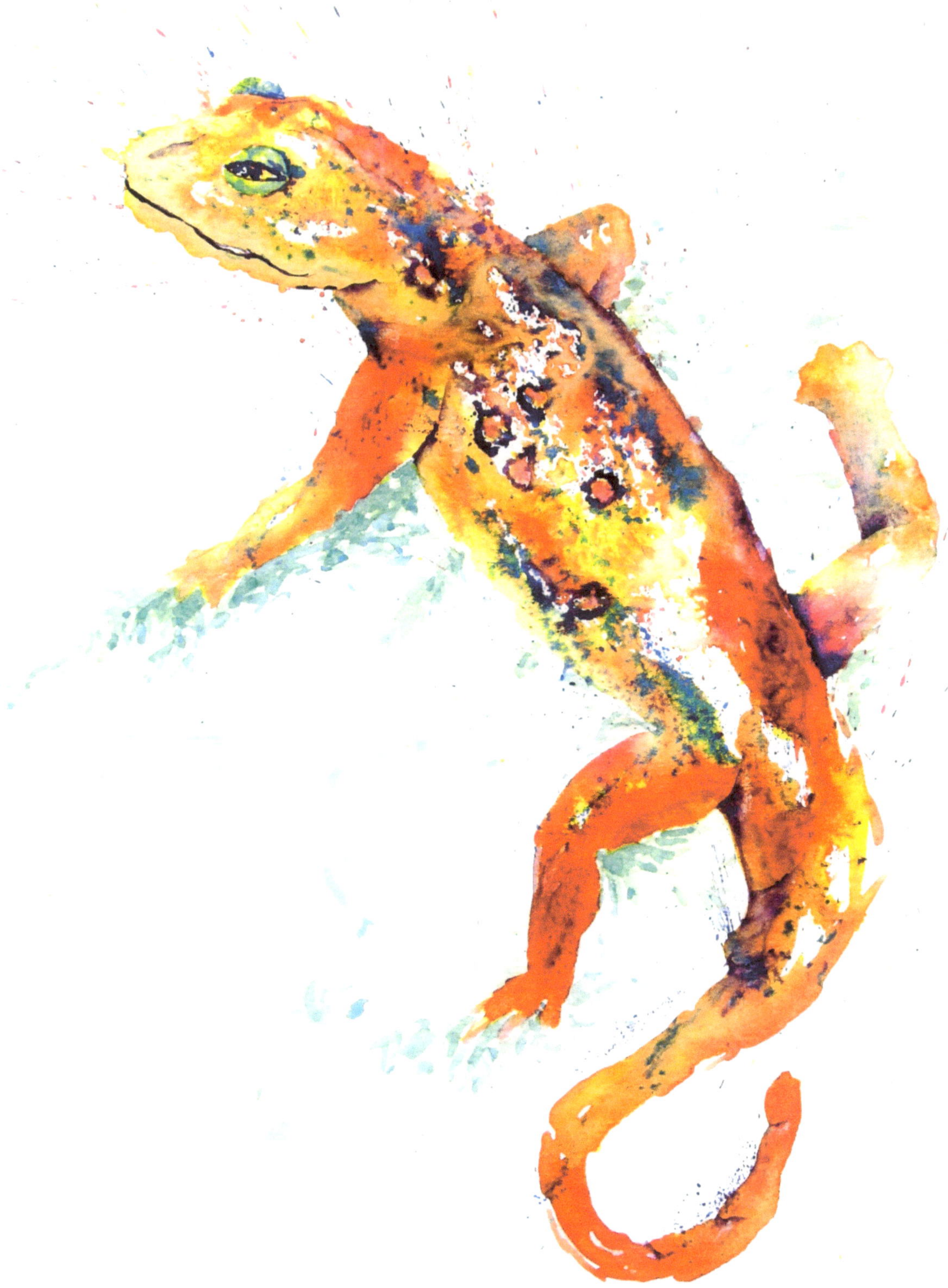

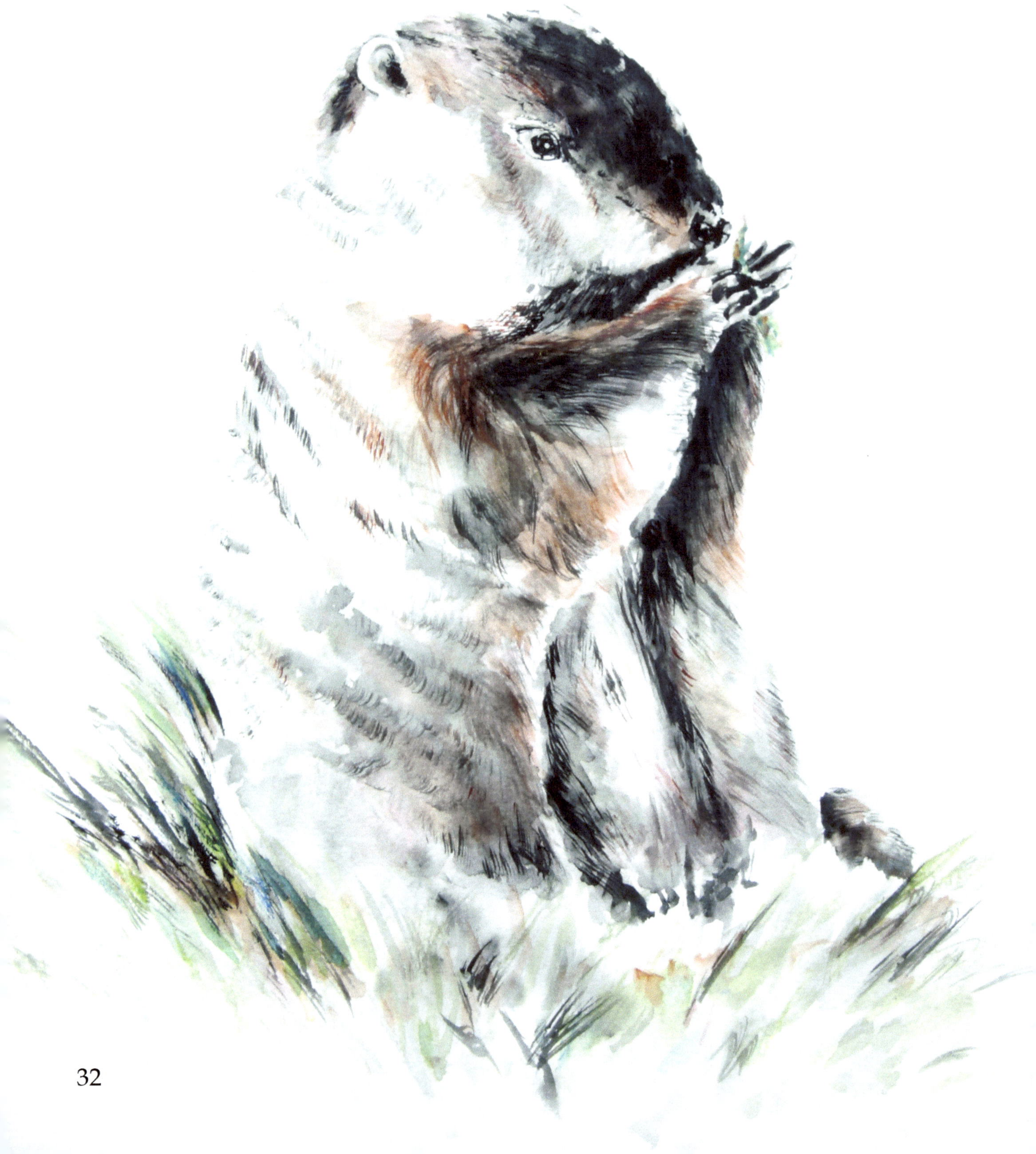

GROUNDHOGS

The groundhogs are eating the peppers.
        Some are nippers and some are grabbers:
the grabbers eat the peppers like a vacuum cleaner;
        they get fatter and the bushes get leaner.
The nippers are neater and eat only a little,
        but they also get fleshy around the middle.
When they finish eating they shimmy and wobble
        out of the peppers—these grabbers and nippers—
to find another crop they can gobble and nibble.

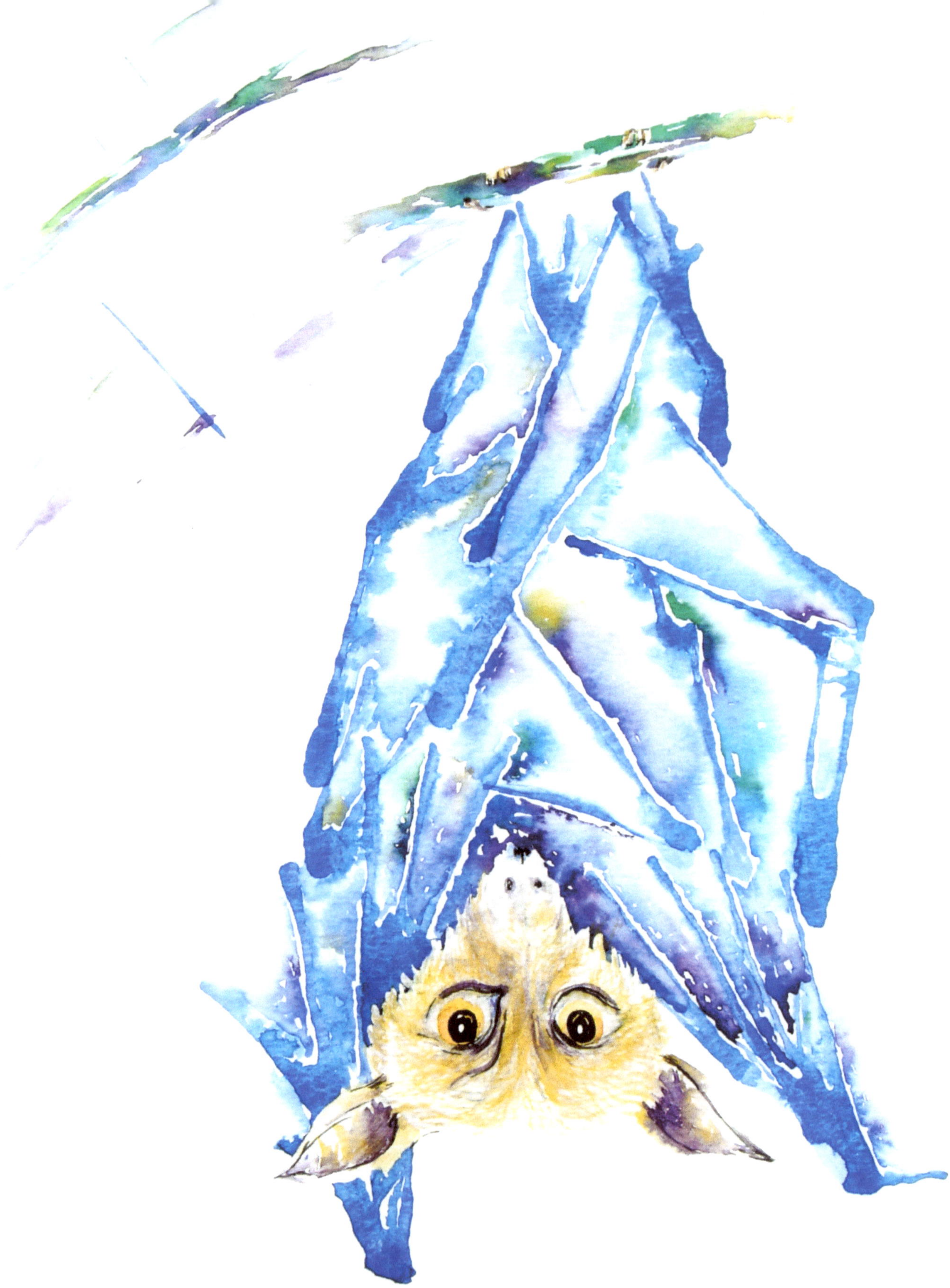

FINCHES AND PORPOISES AND BATS

        Finches
have brief clinches,
        and little finches
that swoop and veer
        with the bigger finches
whose call they hear.

        Porpoises
make noises porpoises
        understand;
they make choices,
        too, that their voices
carry over the sand.

        Bats
talk to themselves: that's
        why they're content
                to stay bats—
but their little chats stop for an instant
        when they meet gnats.

These creatures sing
        and listen
and move with a startling
                zing.
They also glisten.

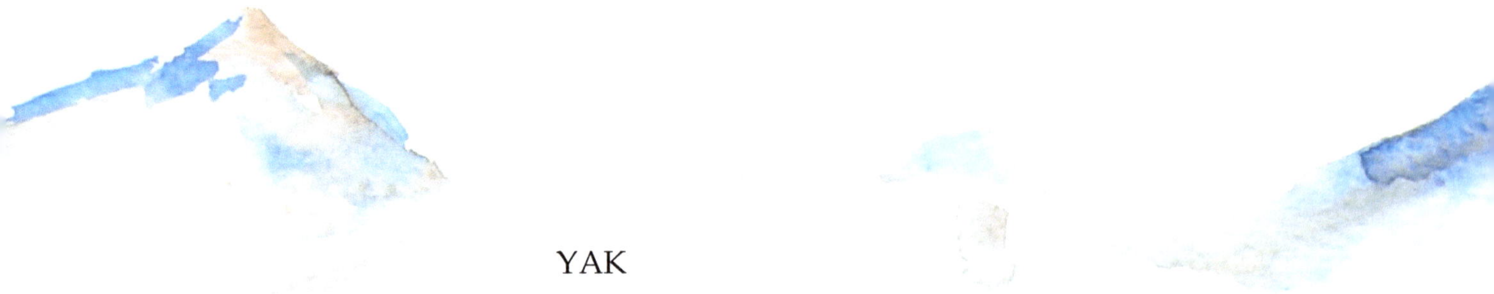

YAK

She's a huge, shaggy mop
with horns, who lives on top
of mountains so high
even birds have to try
extra hard to fly
over their peaks.
But she's quite at home
in the thinnest of air;
she doesn't climb,
she just lives there.
In her carpet of hair
she lumbers around,
taking her time,
covering the ground
she's roamed on for years
dreaming and grazing.

What does she dream of?
Something hair-raising
you can bet, like a haircut
to take all that load off,
and stretches of grass forever
lush green, and some foxglove
and peeswell and clover,
and warm weather all year.

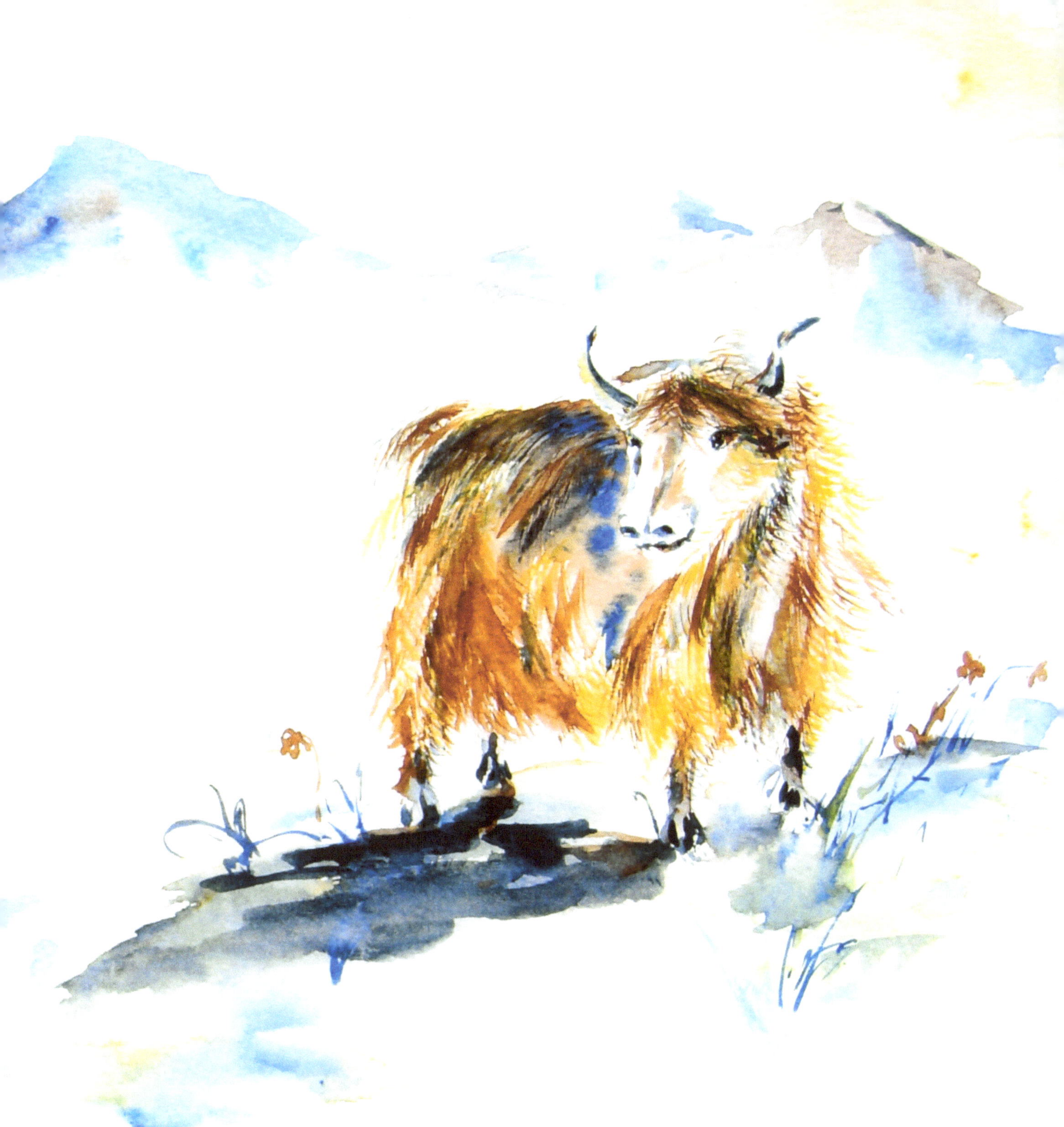

Three

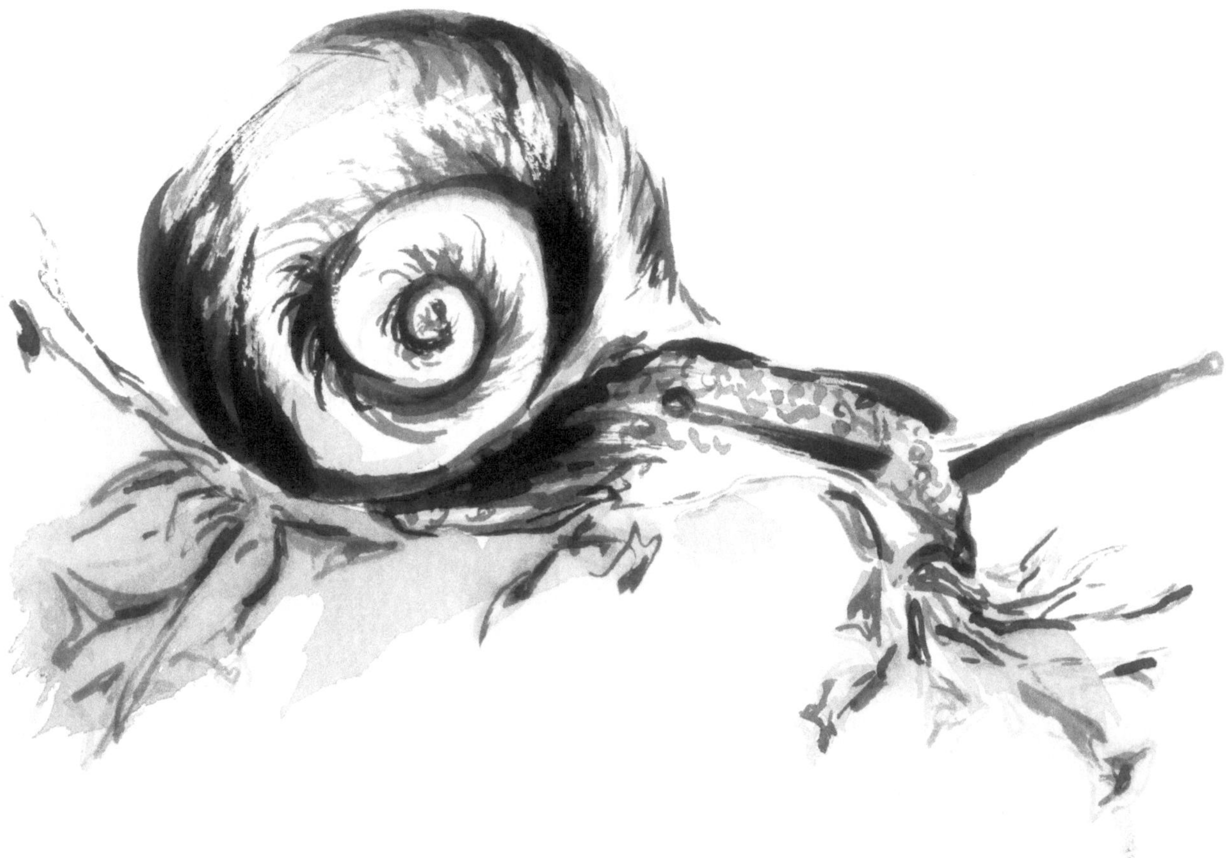

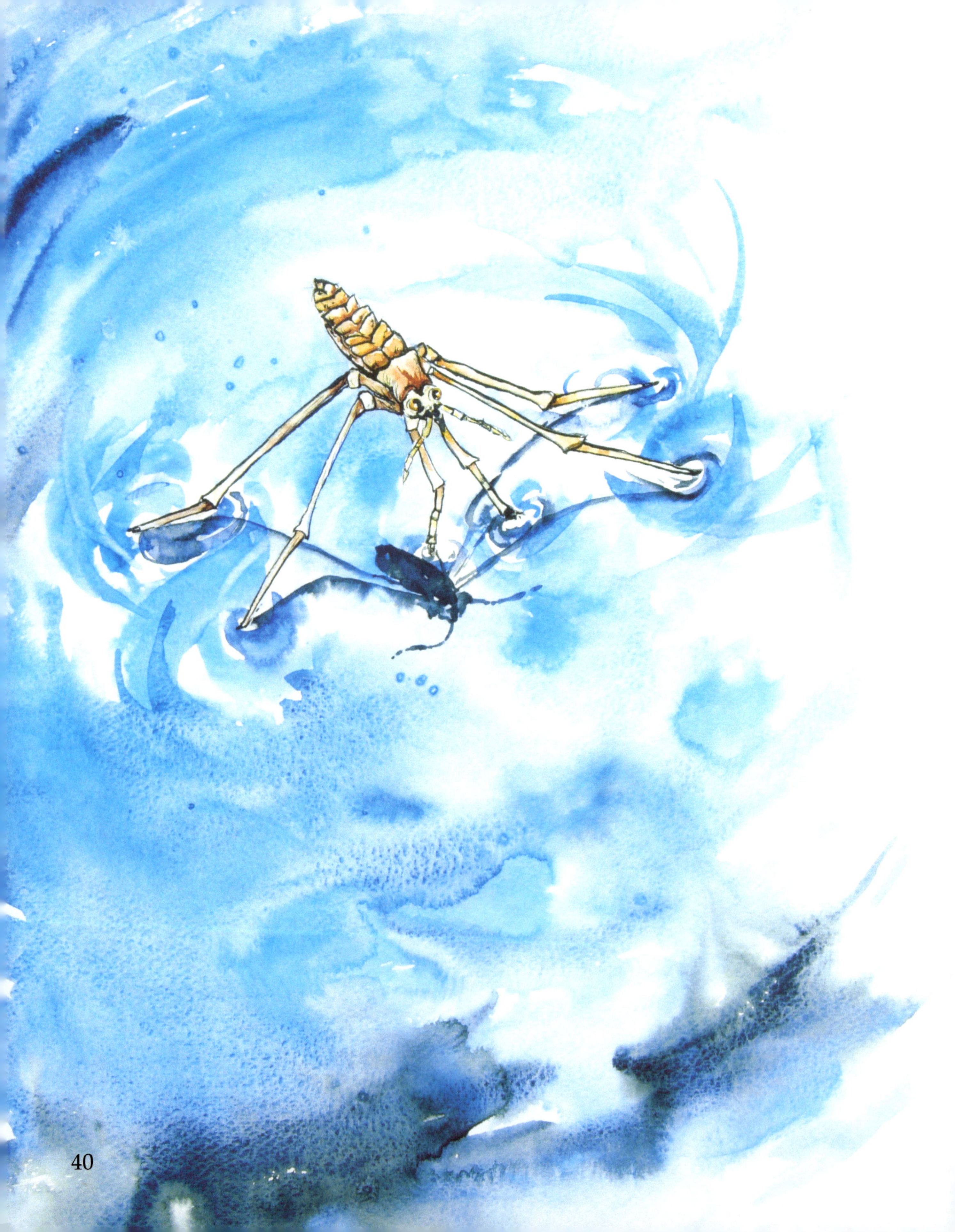

WATER STRIDER

The water strider's
not only a glider:
she jerks and twitches
and then switches
to twitches and jerks.
It always works
to move her from here
to somewhere near
if the water's clear
and calm and flat.
She likes it like that.

But if it's lumpy,
swift and bumpy,
she's not so jumpy:
she's got the knack
of just sitting back
and floating on down,
spinning around:
she comes and goes
as the water flows.
She likes that, too.

She's been to Honolulu
Sheboygan and Boise:
she found them too noisy
and not very pretty.
She left the city.
A born outsider,
the water strider's
a river rider.

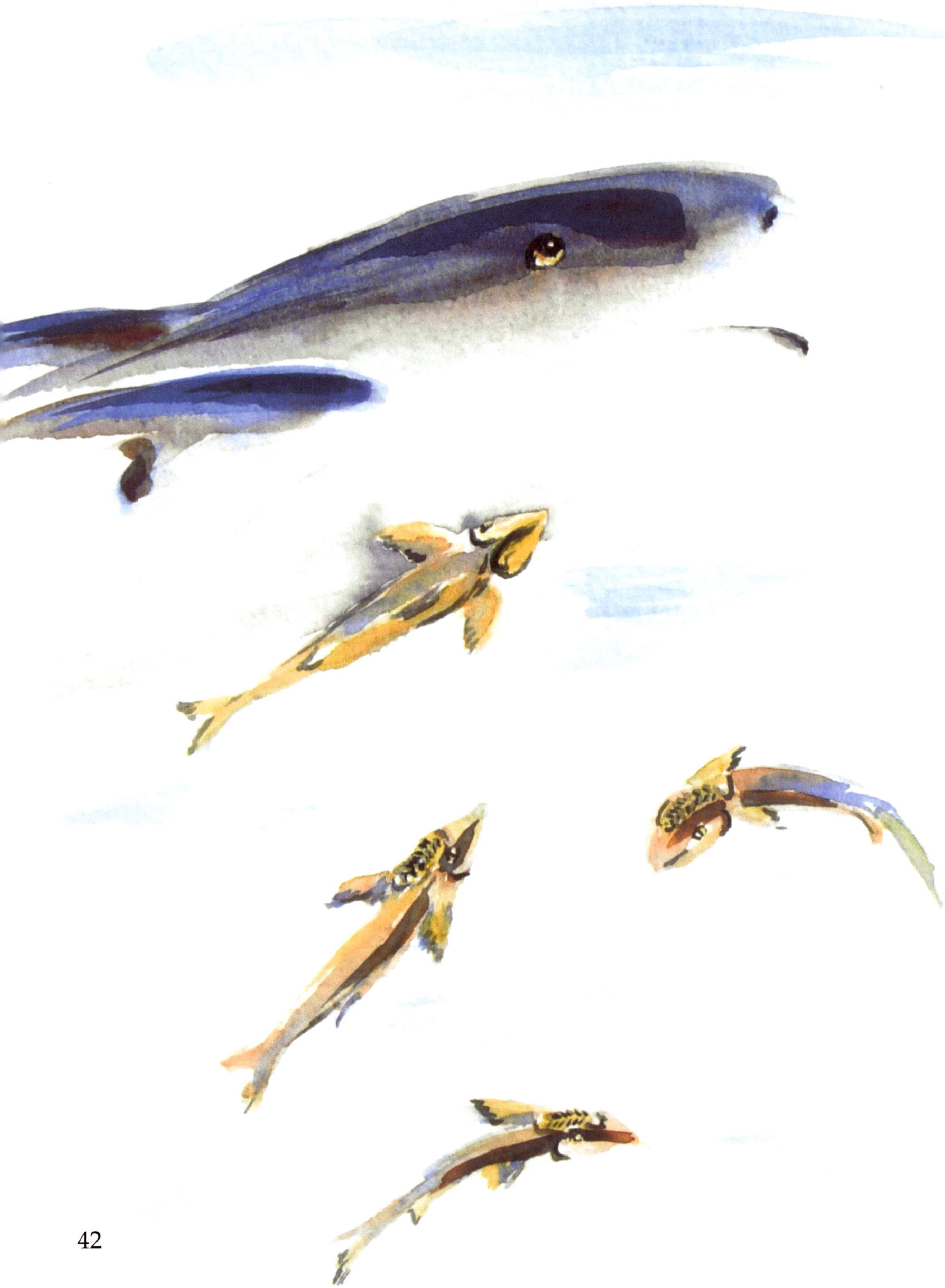

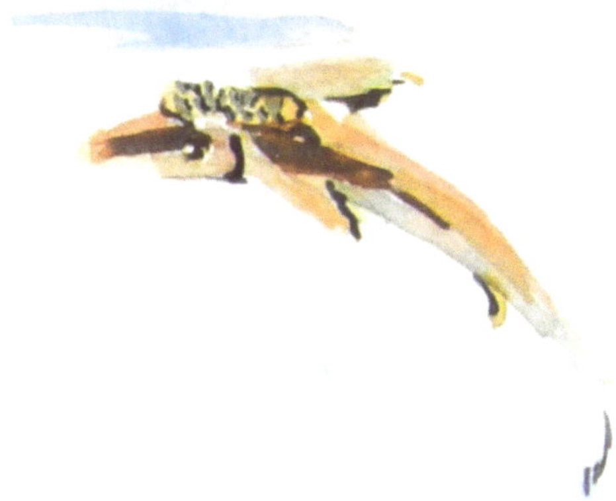

REMORA

His dorsal fin (the fin on top)
has disappeared in the centuries
and been replaced by a suction cup
on his back, behind his head.
When he wants to go from sea to sea
or around the world on a whim,
he attaches himself to a boat
or a bigger fish, like a whale.
It doesn't matter to him
who gives him this long-distance ride.
He doesn't stick out his thumb,
and never fusses with tickets,
or claim checks since he's his own luggage.
It's a convenient way to take trips
if you can scare up a gadget
like his, a free pass from hither
to yon, one world or another.

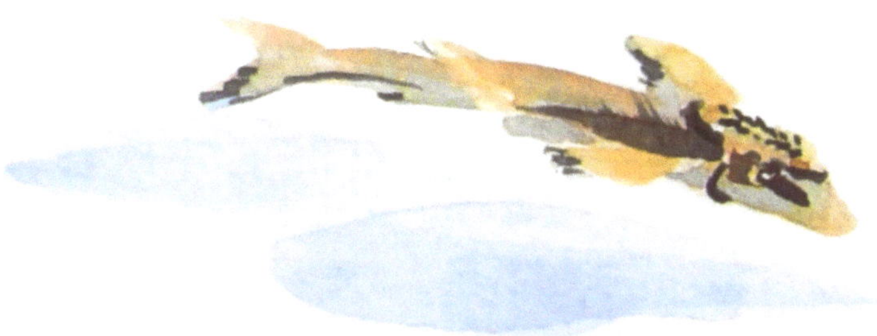

WATER BUFFALO

Coming out of the river
the water buffalo
is a waterfall
from all sides of himself.

Unless he's riled
he's lazy and easy
with all that cascading
and draining and raining
from his watery fur.
He just lets it all slide.

At last when he shakes
himself loose from what's left
of his swim in the river,
if you stand near enough
you'll get a free shower—
a cool way to share
the buffalo's water.

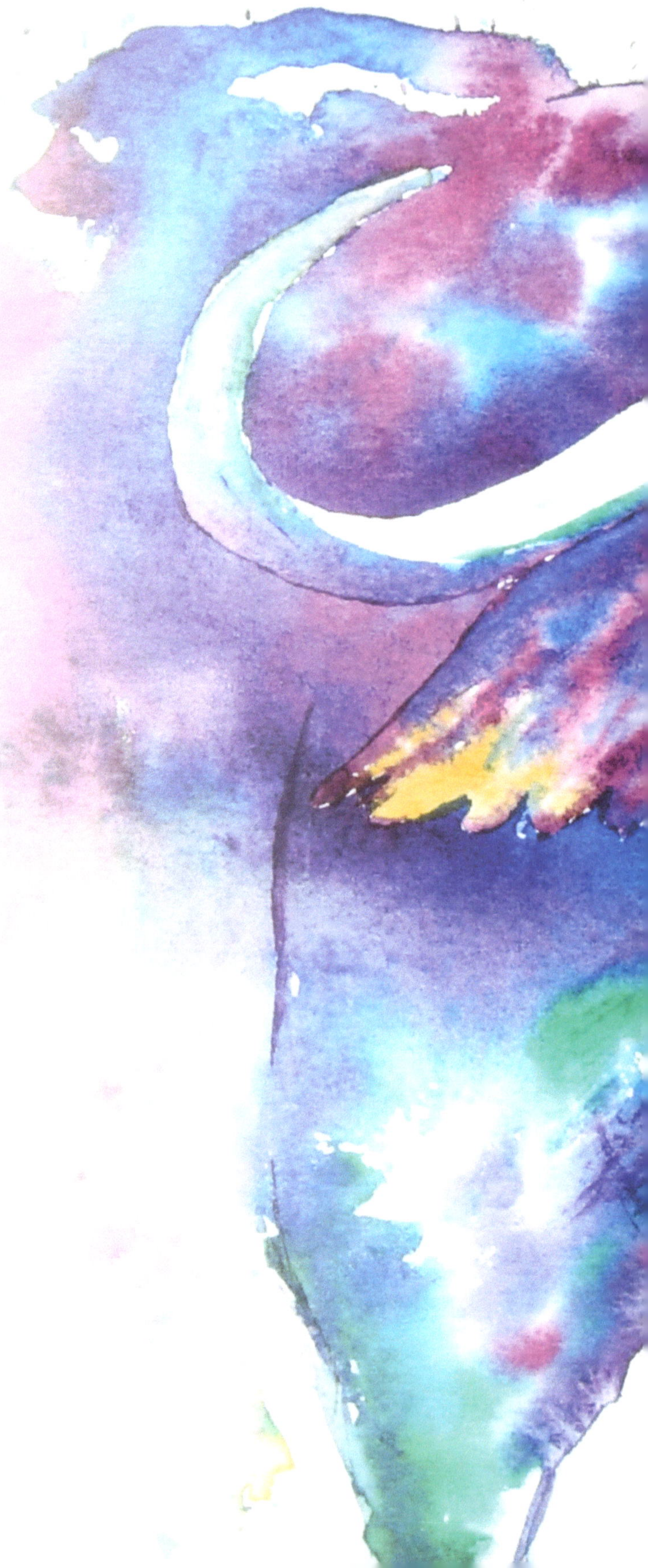

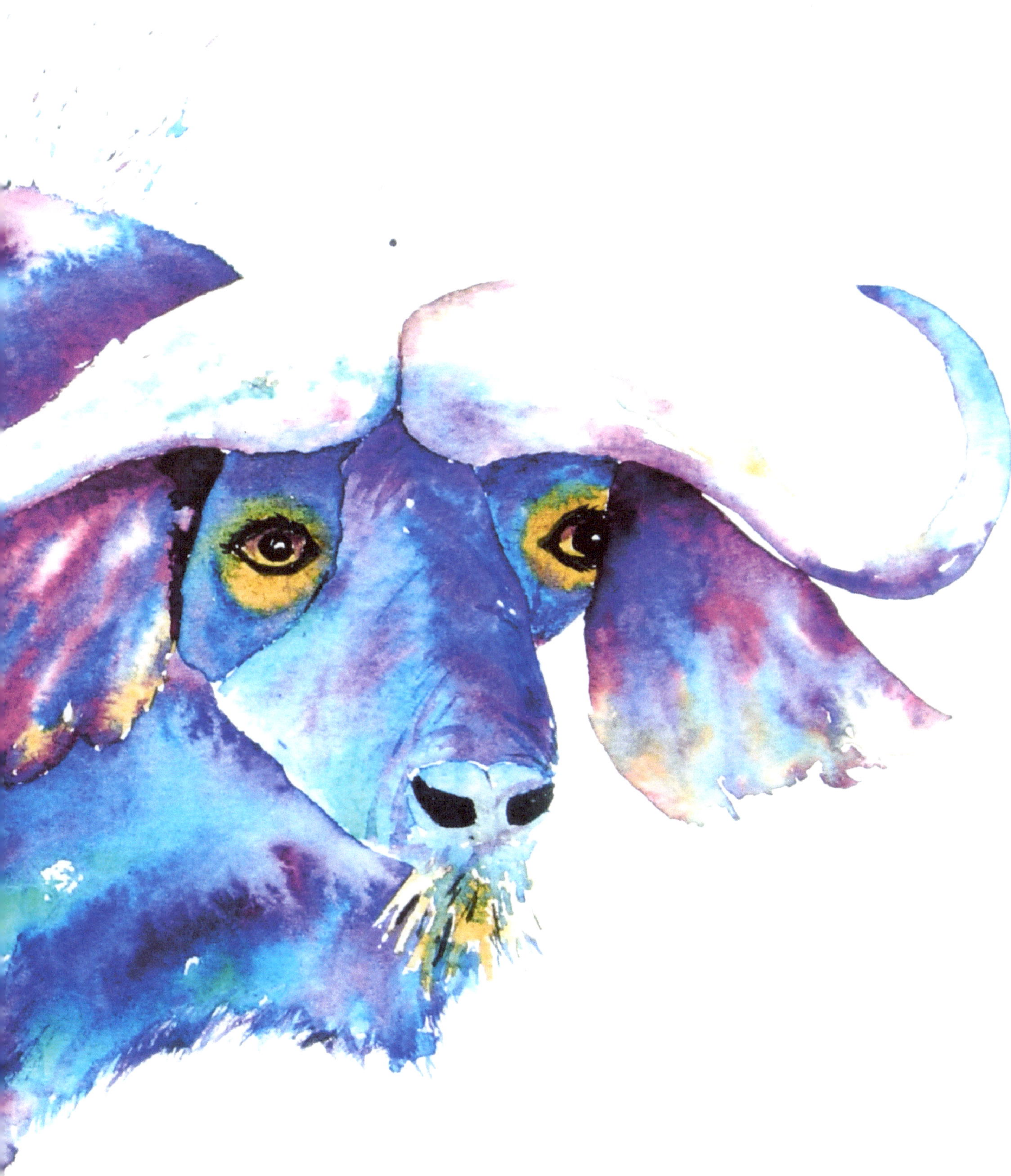

PENGUIN

This dapper gent
can pay the rent
with a flake of snow,
and live on pies
made of layered ice.
He's on the go
from November to April
when the days are long—
in fact, it's one day!
He slipslides his way
down snowhill and icehill
like a bird on the wing.

Ooops, sorry... forgot:
the penguin is earthbound,
or icebound, or snowbound—
he can't fly, in short.
(But suppose, oh suppose,
that the right wind blows!)
He's a whiz in the water,
like a seal, or an otter,
a sleek sub-zero
kind of bird hero.
In our planet's downunder
he celebrates wonder,
using those wings
(that aren't really wings)
for applause, of all things!

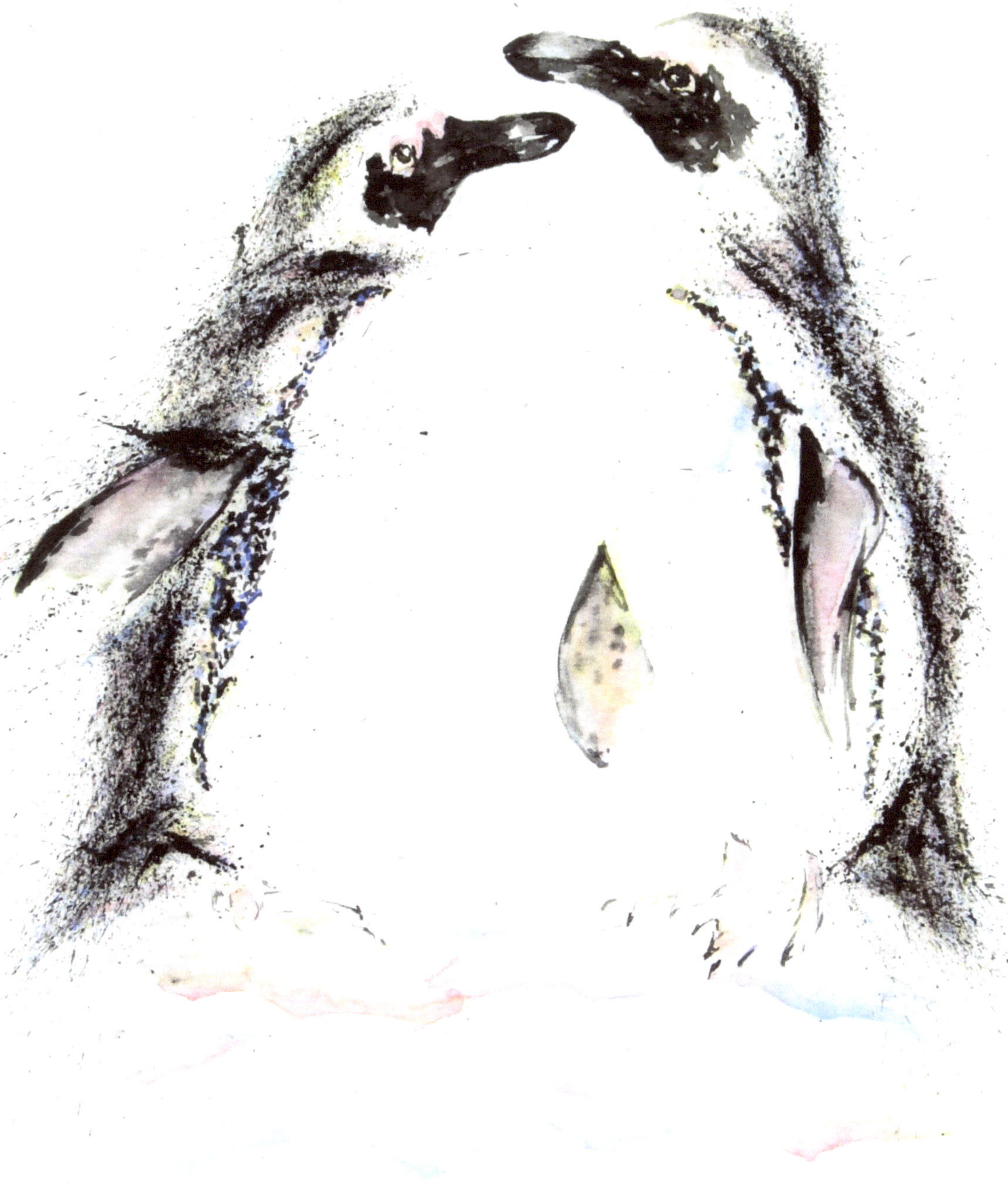

WHALES

The whales
have been yelling their tails
off,

pouting and spouting
great bowls
of air out of their air holes,

flipping and flopping
so full of whale they give motion
to the ocean—

great, gray sloping
and thriving, and I bet you supposed
they were just diving.

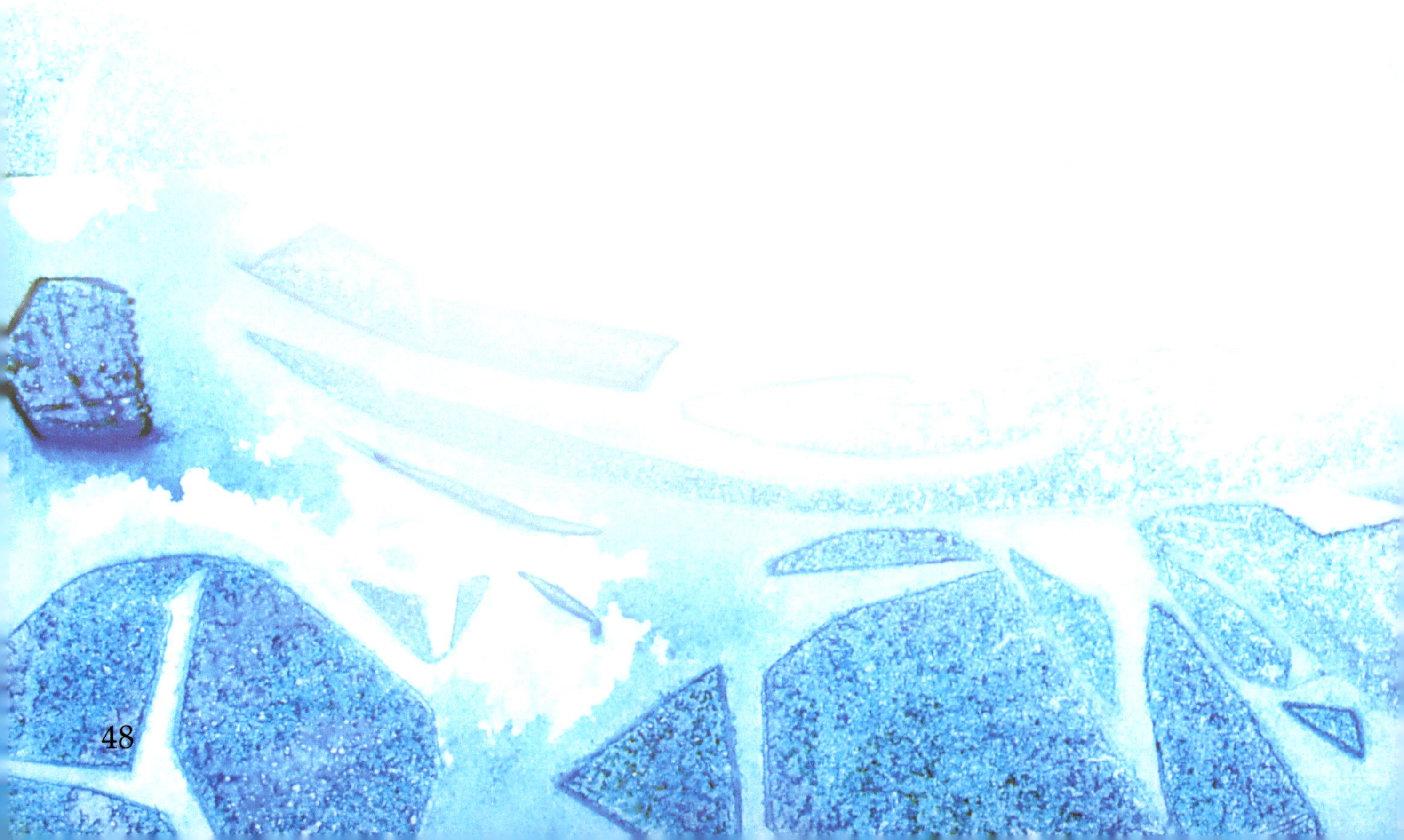

ELECTRIC EEL

The electric eel had one big wish:
to swim around like other fish—
not to curl, or slide, or shimmer,
not to brighten, and grow dimmer,
not to slip into small places
and never meet with other faces,
not to be left out of races
because she won them every time,
not to wriggle through the slime
down on the bottom where it's cold,
not to grow big, and then grow old
coiling herself up, fold on fold.

Her friend the clam inquired, "What's wrong?"

"I wish, at least, I weren't so *long*."
"Next thing, you'll want to sing a song,"
the clam said. "Listen, you've got style.
What other fish can make a smile
out of herself by curving? Cripes,
you were *made* to sneak through pipes,
the deep-sea slalom's your event.
When God said, 'Here's my filament'
you're the creature that He meant—
a lamppost moving through the dark,
your grandpa guided Noah's ark.
If we had bridges in the sea
you'd be the only one for me.
So stretch on out and love it, sport.
It's ordinary being short."

The eel curved up and made a grin
and licked her tail and stroked her chin:
"You're a good friend," she told the clam.
"From now on I'll be just what I am."

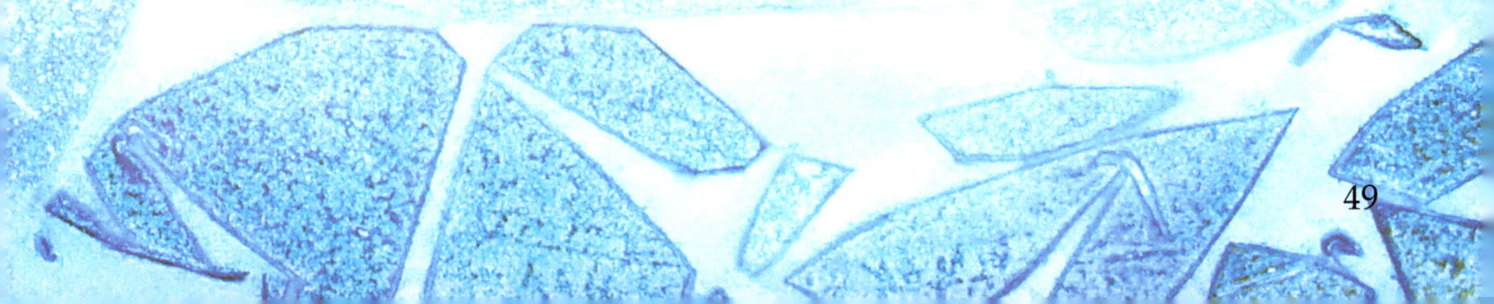

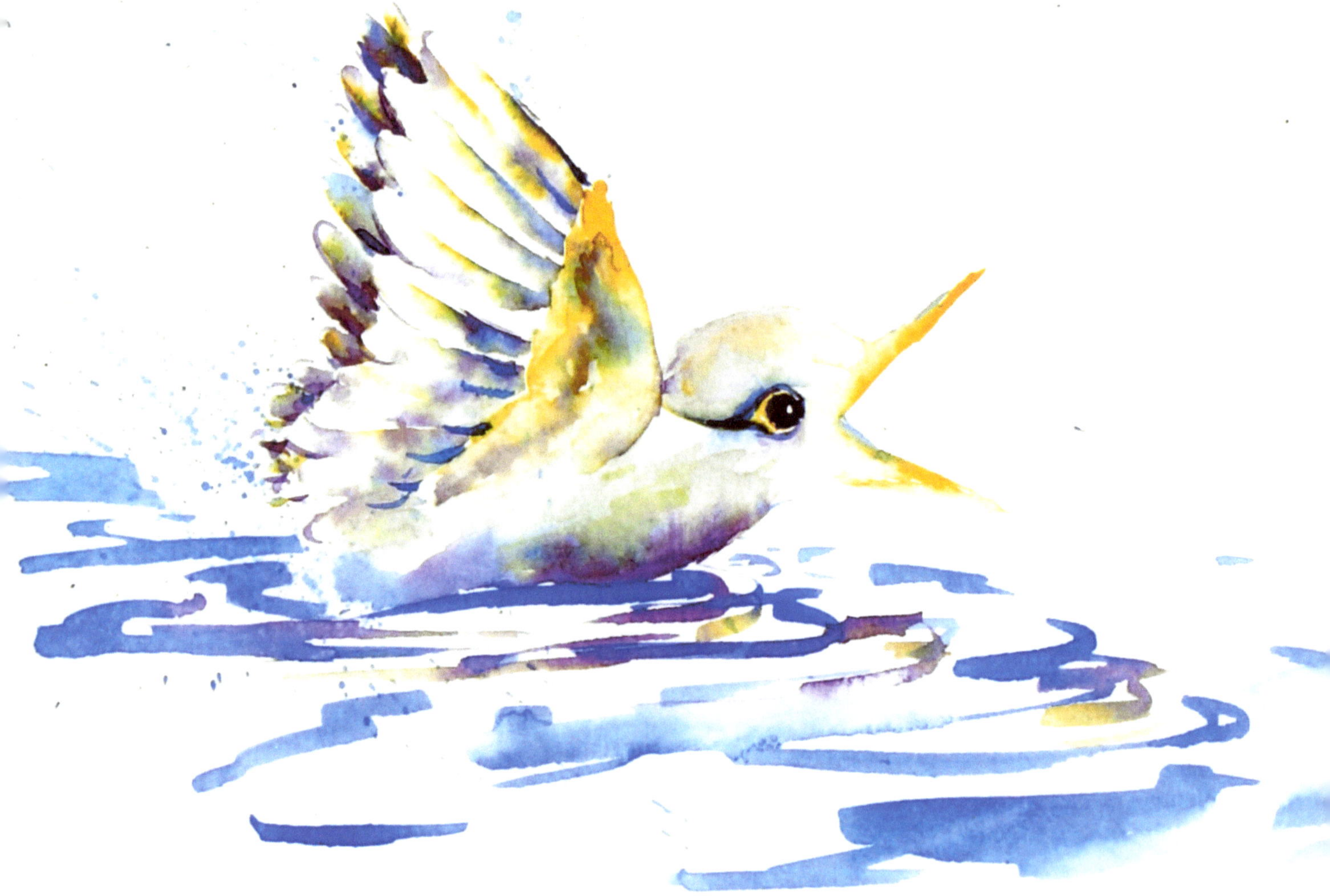

WATER OUZEL

The water strider's
a river rider,
but the ouzel can go
where the water's flow
is darker and deeper—
he can walk on the bottom!
He'll be floating along
on the river's surface
and, suddenly diving,
he'll—POOF—disappear.

If there're snacks down there
you can bet he's got 'em.
If you're watching from shore,
though, you wonder about him.
He's been down a long time.
Has he forgotten the air?
Is he tangled in grasses
of which there are masses
in the murk underneath?
Has he got enough breath
to endure this submersion?

Just when it seems certain
our worst fears are confirmed
that he'll be gone forever,
he emerges unharmed—
off there—way down river
almost out of sight,
shaking the water drops
out of his feathers.
He's come out on top.
There's no greater delight
than the feeling we get
when our lost ones recover
and come back from the night.

Four

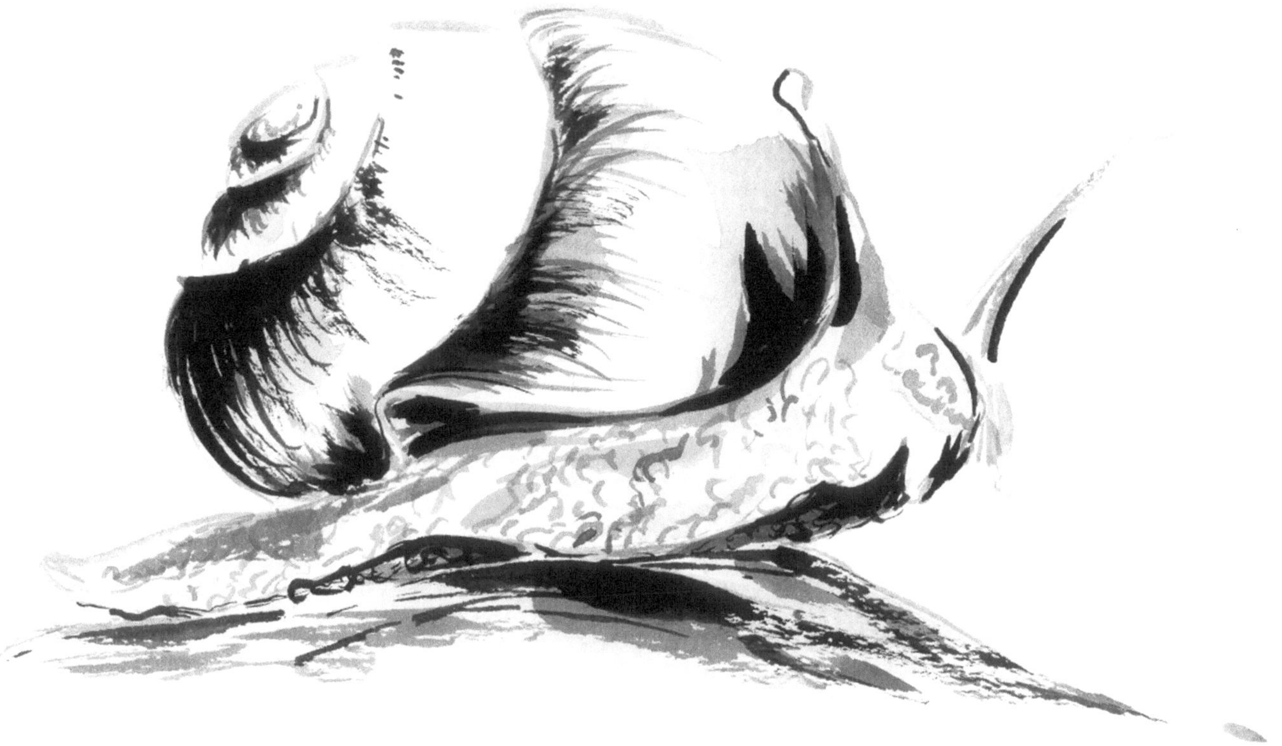

HUGE BALLOON

There's something in
          a huge balloon.
What could it be,
It's got to be large
or it would get lost
and wander around
in this monster balloon
like a fish in the sea.
Perhaps it's a barge,
or a lonesome wolfhound,
or a mountain of moss.
Or would it have to be round
to fit in the balloon,
like a ball or a globe,
or a swollen ear lobe?

It couldn't be birds—
they'd peck holes in the sides.
Could it be a bassoon?
or a group of bassoons
arranged in a ring
and tooting a tune?
Could the music get caught
in the skin of its air?
It stays silent in there!

One thing's for sure,
about this balloon—
It's a world of its own.
But that still doesn't tell
what it carries inside.
Is it secrets, or plans
for the future, or a place to hide?
Or a stack of tin cans,
or a bear with a bell,
or a bouquet of roses
for a giant's girlfriend?

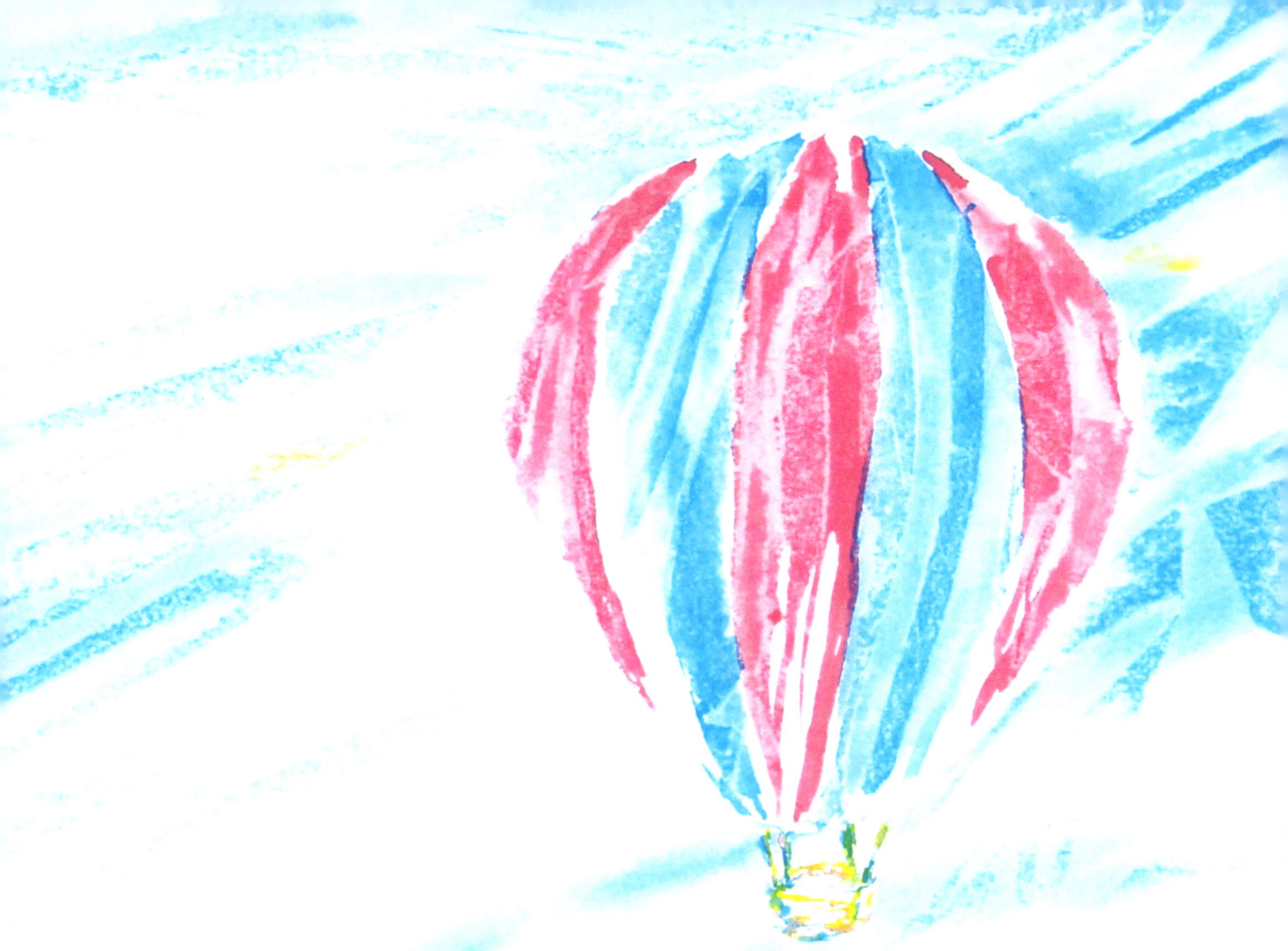

There's never an end
to the things we can pull
from our bag of supposes,
the balloon in the mind.
In there we can find
the heaviest care
that brings us to sighing
and fill it with air
and send it off flying!

SAND FIDDLER

The fiddler crab
whenever she plays
has picked up the habit
of playing sideways.

Her favorite music
is classical jazz
with drums in the background
to give it pizazz.

The anemone thinks
that she plays very well
but the crotchety clam
always slams down his shell.

She sometimes gives concerts
for herds of blue whales;
they munch buttered popcorn
and wriggle their tails.

The tuna, however,
say she comes on too loud;
they can't understand
how she draws such a crowd.

Someday, when she's old,
she may suffer with gout;
her legs will get creaky
and her feet will give out.

Then how will she manage?
It's really no riddle;
she'll saddle a seahorse
and continue to fiddle.

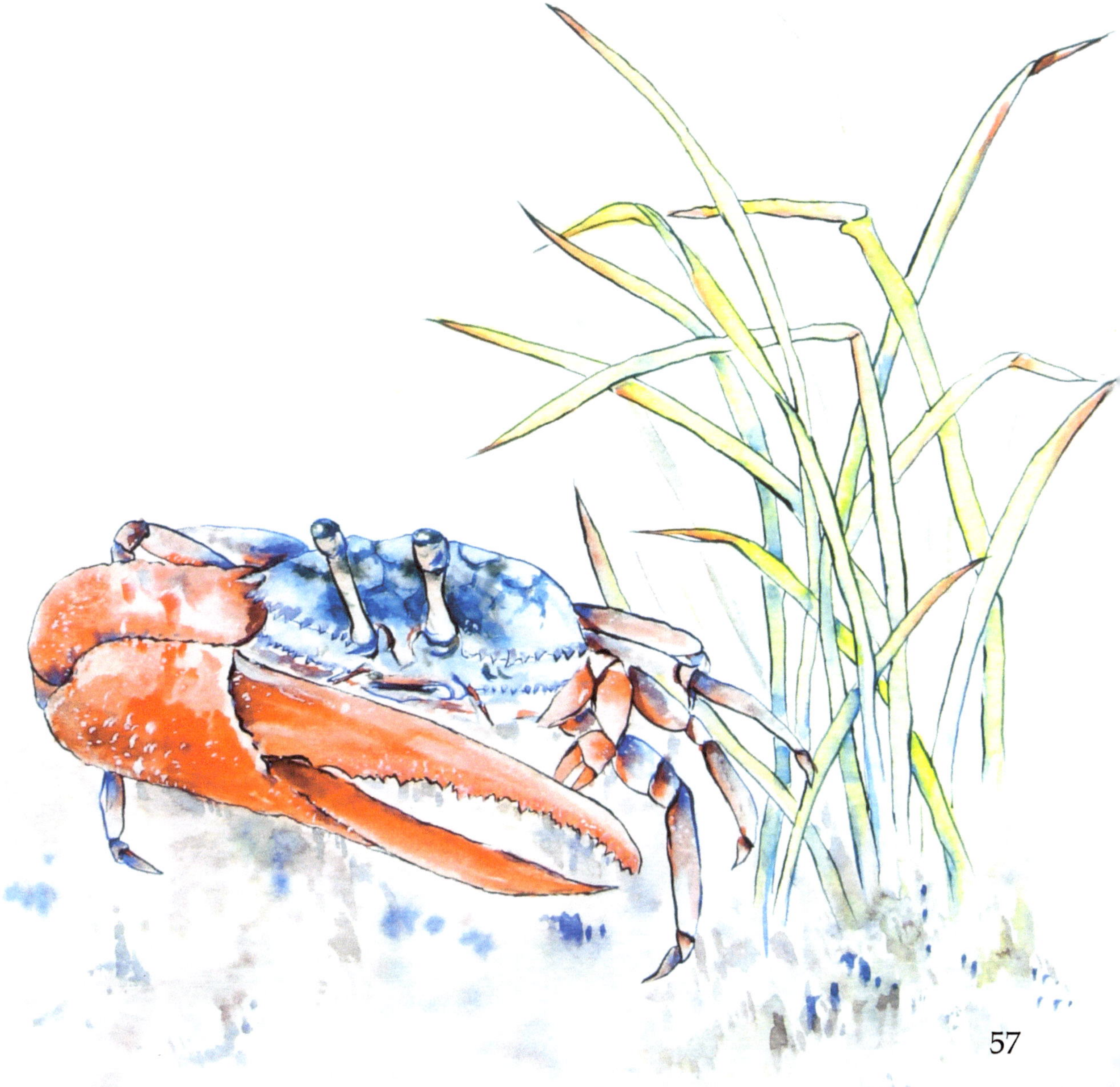

IGUANA

When the iguana
takes her sauna
she doesn't sweat,
she just gets wet
between her toes;
and then she knows
it's time to take
a dip in the lake,
where it's as cold
as the North Pole.

Then she dries
her back and thighs,
her armored shins
and chuckly chins
on fresh palm leaves.
She puffs and heaves
up the rocky hill
(as iguanas will
if they live on top)
to her antique shop.

She sells old shoes
and yesterday's news,
rusty tin cans
and frying pans
crusted with grease,
stale strudel by the piece,
mildewed comics
and wormy sticks.
She keeps all that junk
in a steamer trunk
with her cashmere sweater.
Business is better
than you might think.

She stays in the pink;
sometimes she works right
into the night
on her bamboo mat.
When you work like that
(like our iguana)
you *need* a sauna.

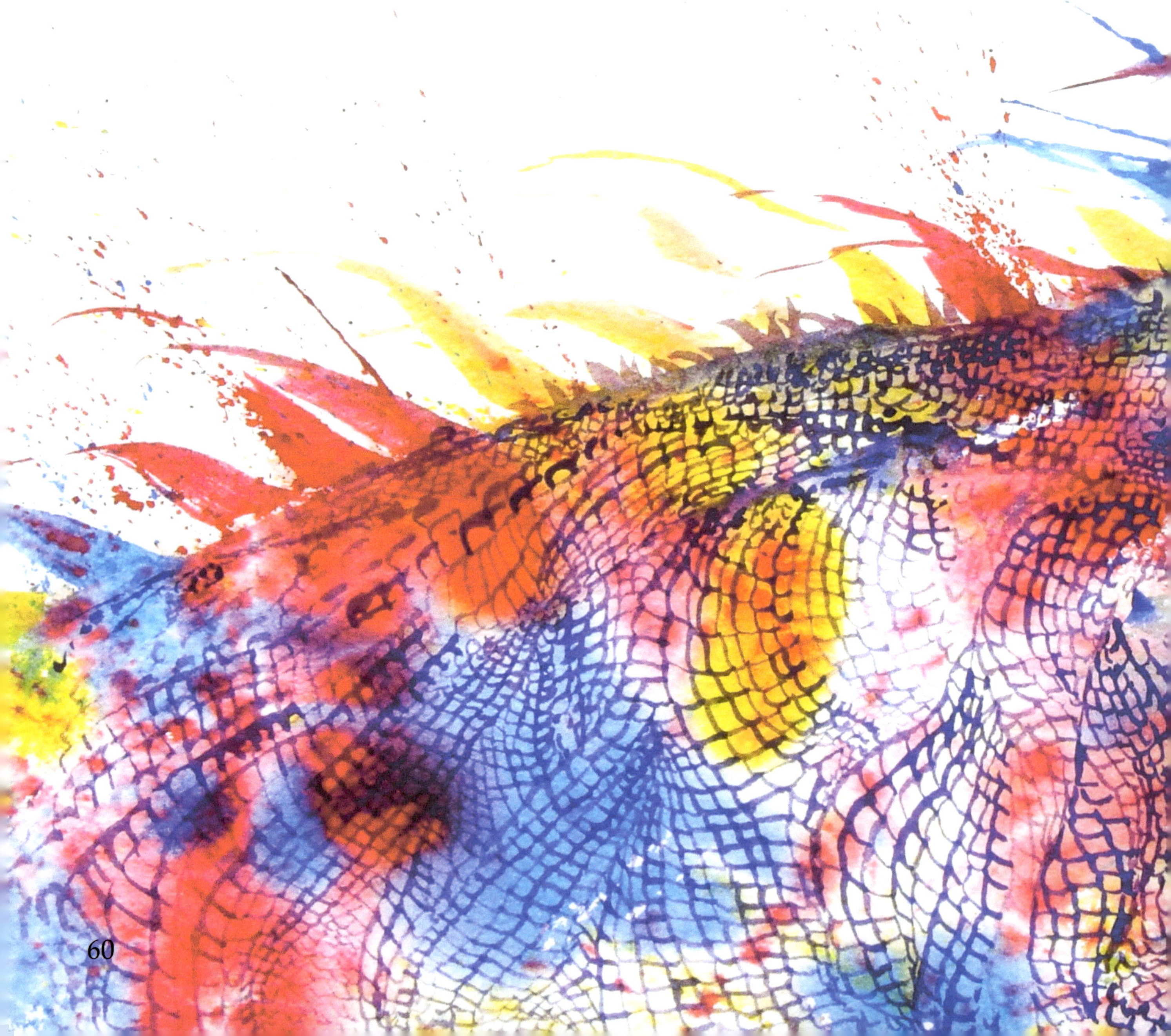

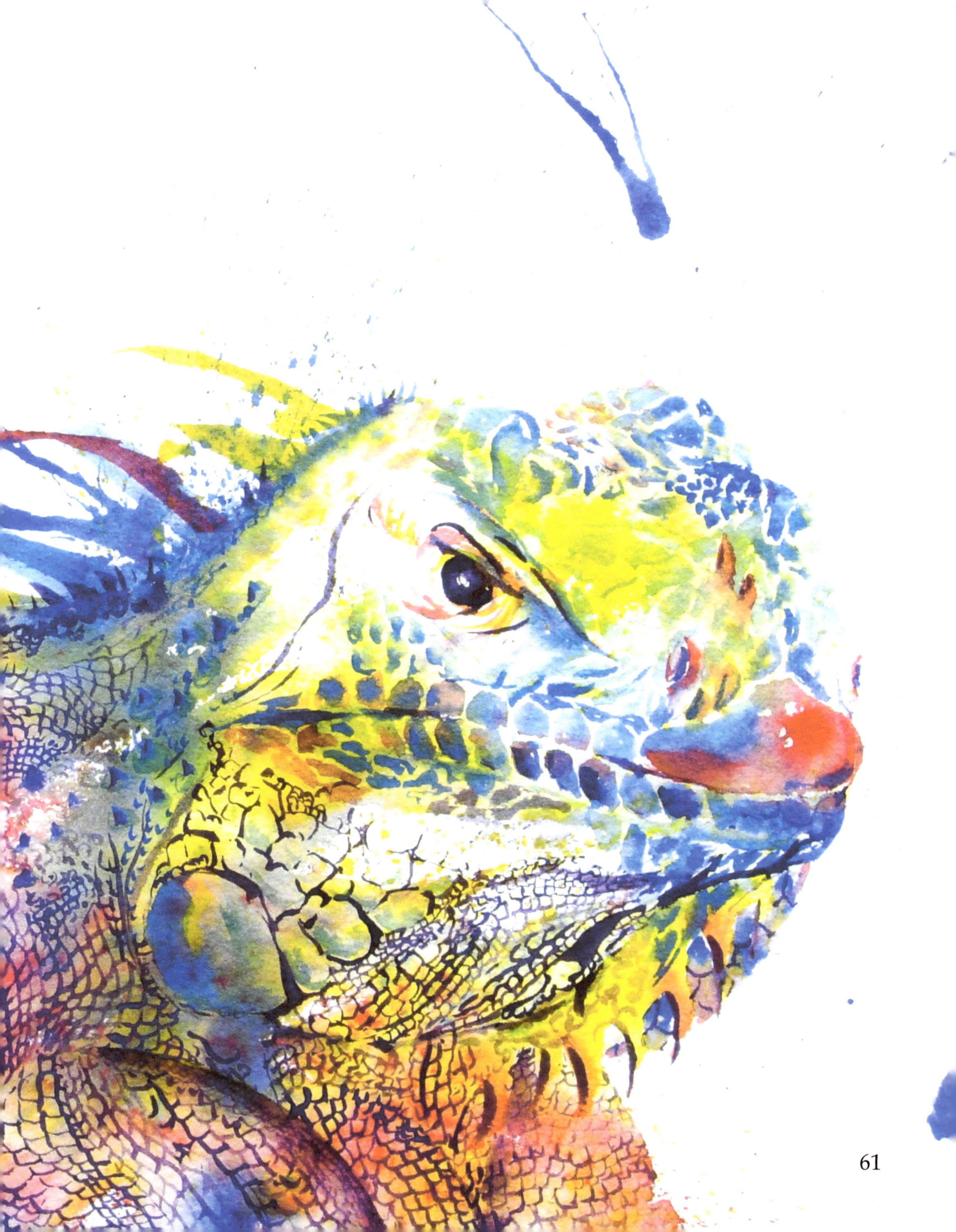

CROCODILE

The crocodile doesn't seem to care
where he puts his evening wear.
He keeps it in his bottom drawer
or stuffed behind the closet door.
He may go out and buy some more.
When he puts on his casual clothes
he wears a red sock on his nose
and knitted thimbles on his toes.
He's not as crude as you suppose.
He pops a nightcap on his head,
with tassles, when he goes to bed,
and in the morning replaces that
with a candy-striped top hat.
The croc's a king of mix and whim—
he wears whatever pleases him.

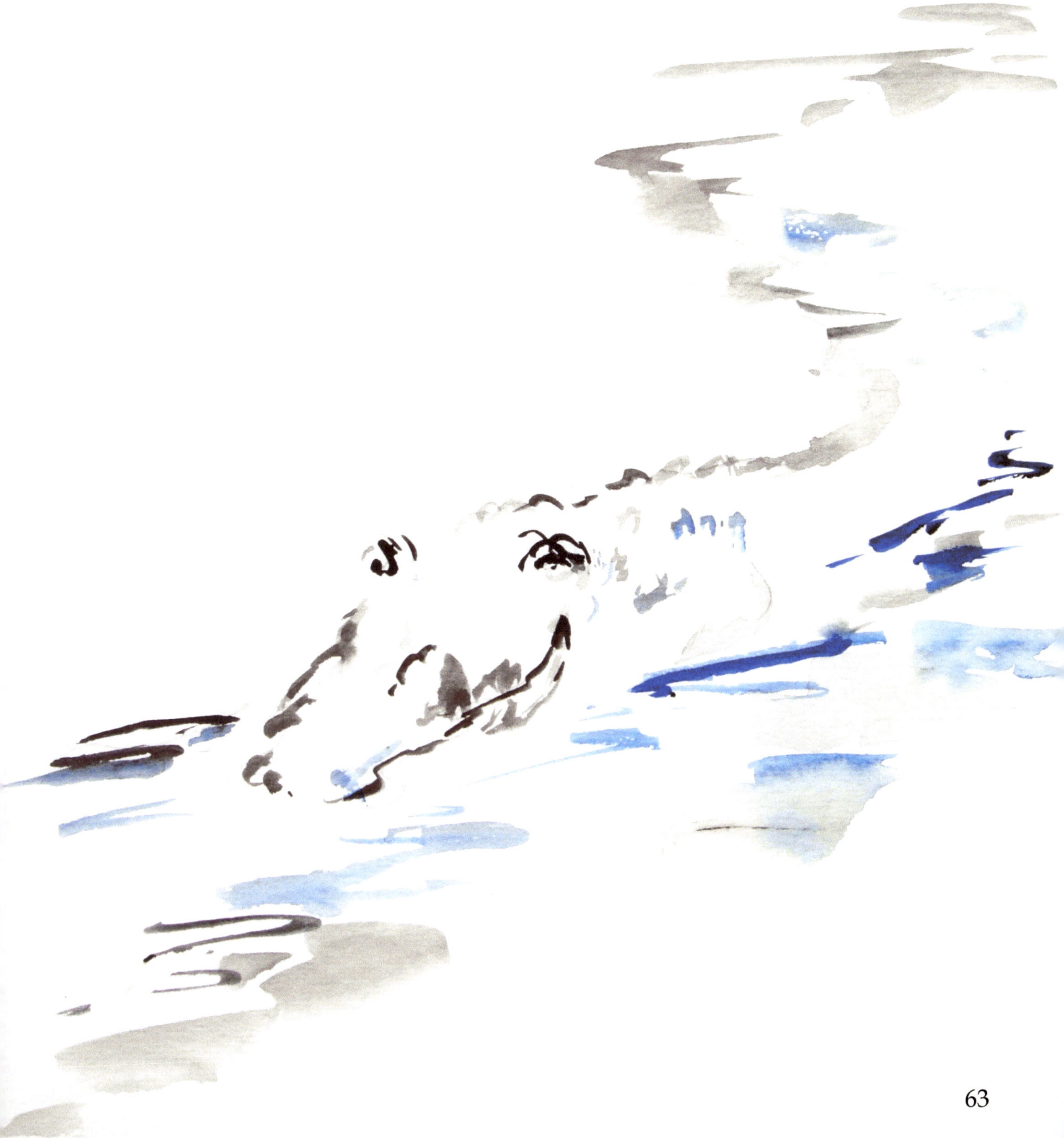

LEMUR

The lemur's ghost is out of sight,
which means that you can't see him, right?

But if you could you'd find he keeps
a yellow frisbee where he sleeps.

The thing about it is, he rides
upon his frisbee where it glides.

He skinned his head when he was six
by crashing in a pile of bricks,

upside down. You see, he dipped
while flying low, and flipped.

When he dines at half past eight
his frisbee is his dinner plate;

once when he landed in the sea
he used it as a water ski;

nobody saw him speeding by,
white cheeks apuff, and tail up high.

He wears a fancy yellow hat
(his frisbee!) to the laundromat

and turns it over when he's through
to carry home his wife's muu muu.

Oh yes, he has a wife, but she
is as invisible as he.

She loves him lots, but from her notch
high in the tree she hates to watch

him frisbee skyward all alone
while she talks on the telephone

trying to find a workman who
can build a frisbee fit for two.

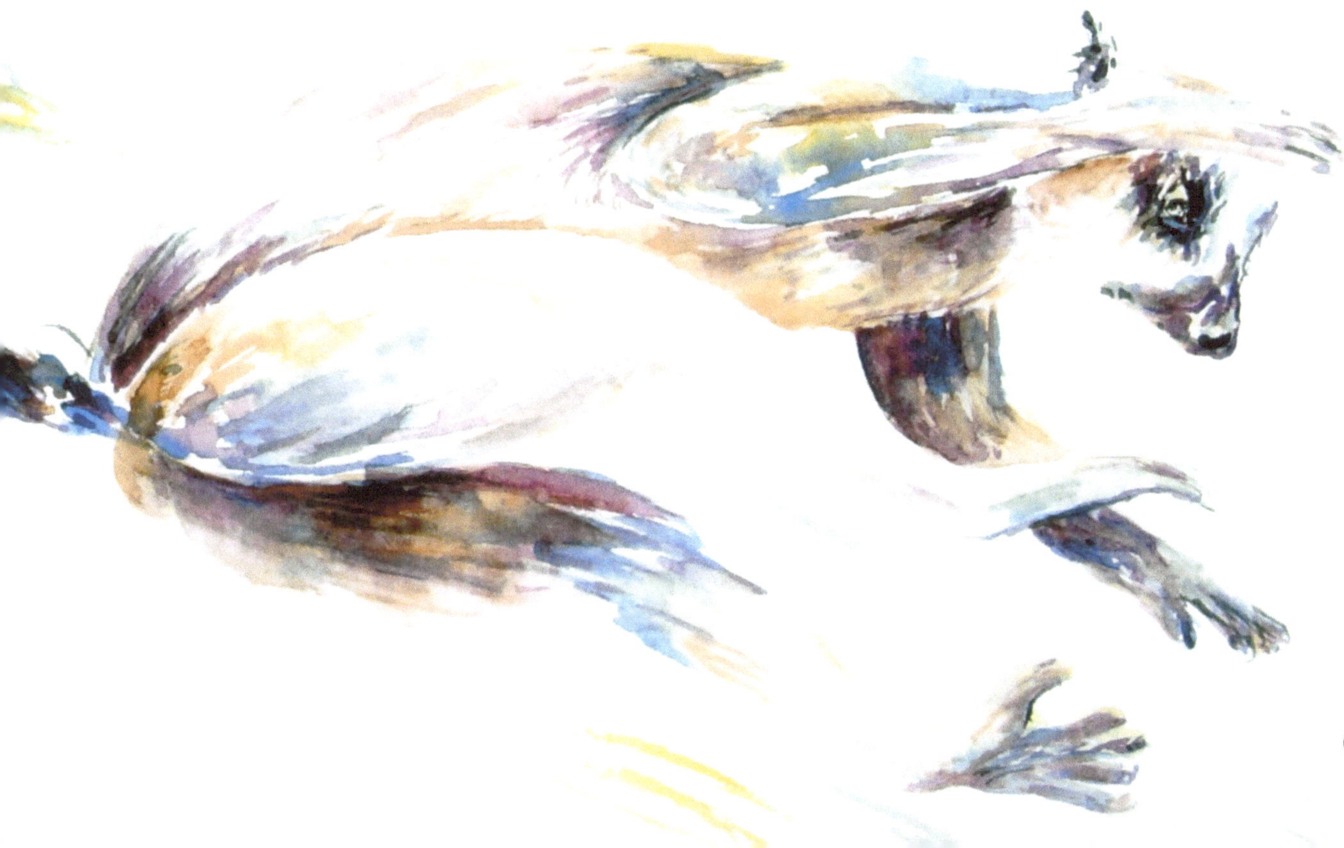

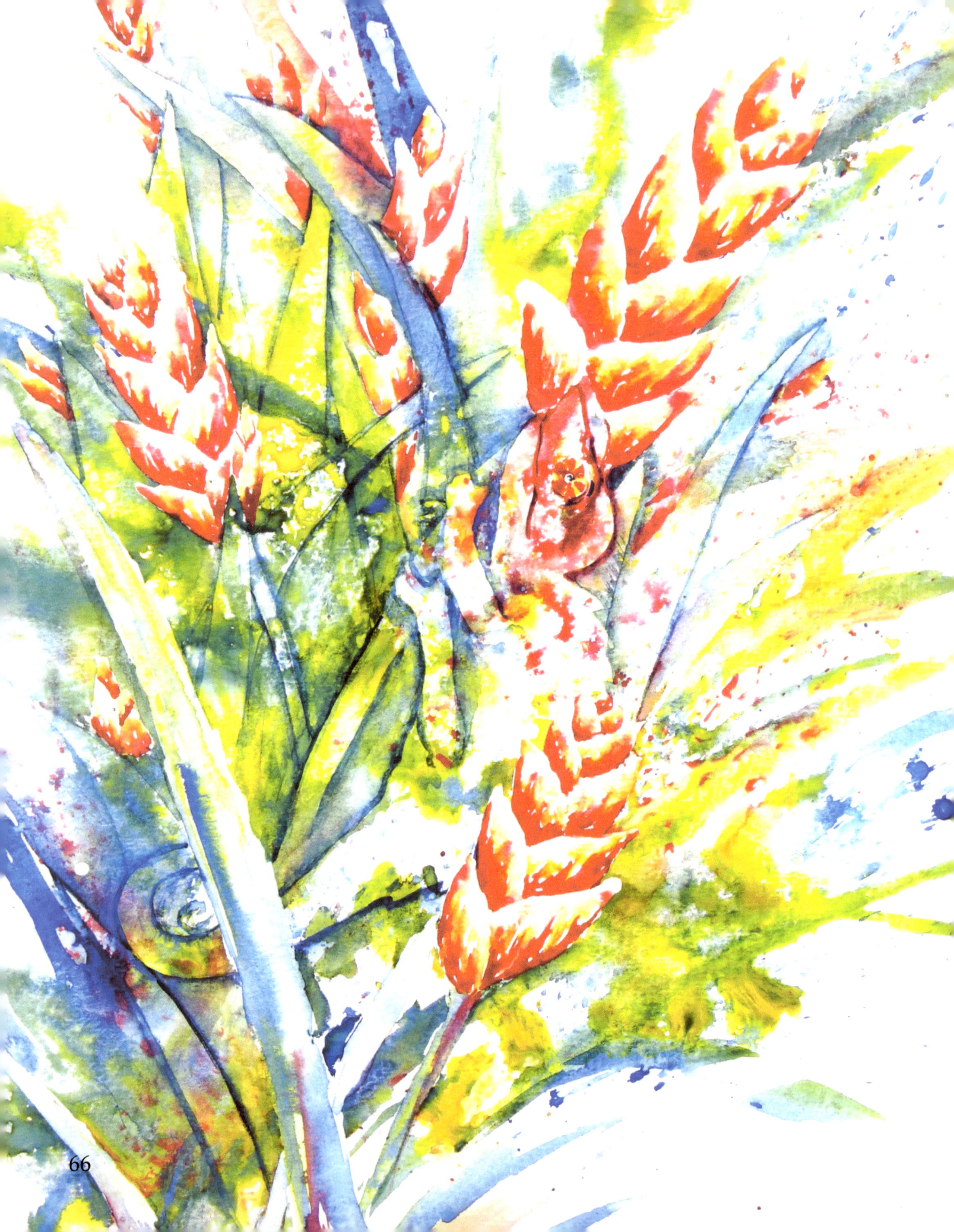

CHAMELEON

He's a patchwork quilt
of colors that shift
and slide into others
when he wants them to.
He has the gift
of blending into
where he finds himself:
out on a twig
among leaves, or atilt
on the edge of a shelf
of stone on a cliff.
He's not very big
but he has more surprises
in his store of disguises
than a magician on stage.
He creates his own cage
and escapes from it, too!

But changing his color
isn't just a maneuver
to hide in the open
and avoid being eaten.
This cover's *more* cover,
an act that's much harder:
over and over, and over,
from lip to tail tip
he makes himself up.

Five

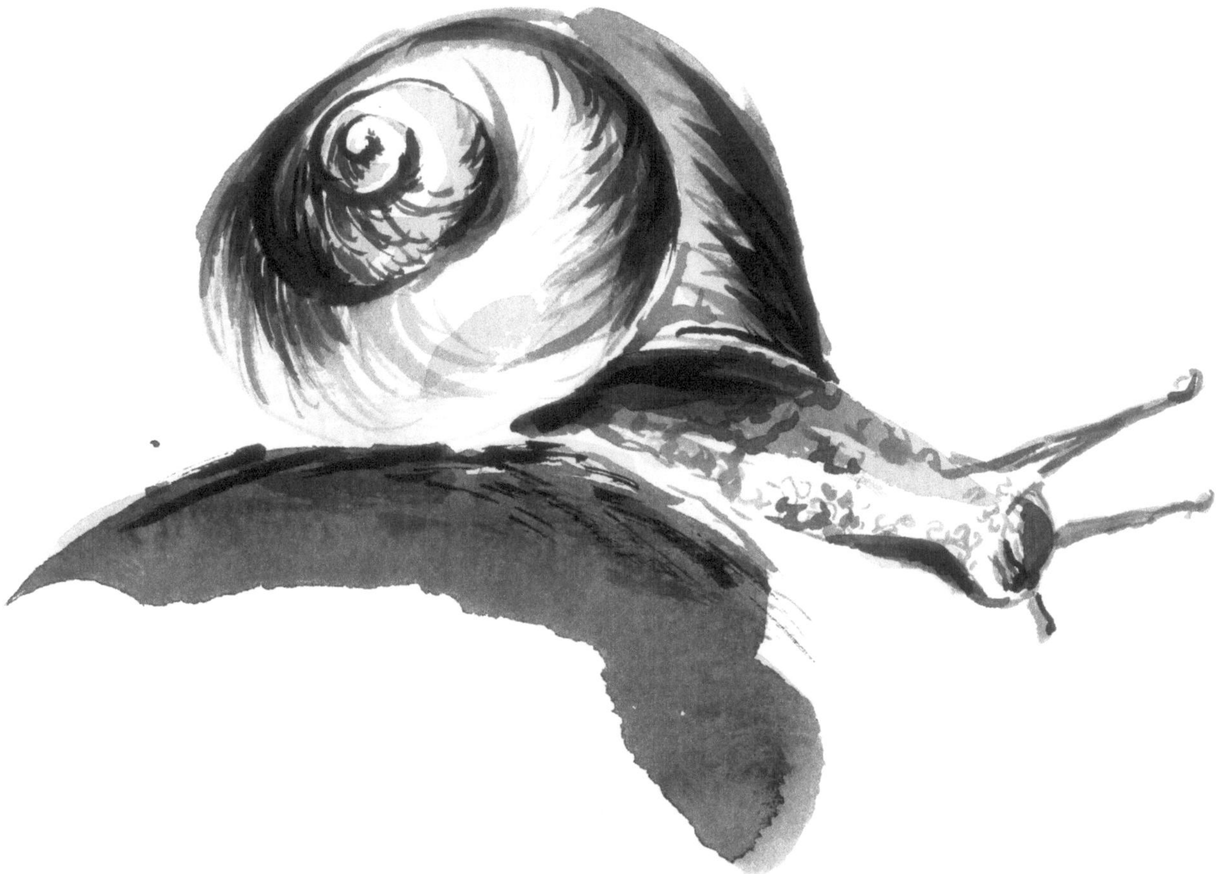

UNICORN

The unicorn
was never born.

He quietly formed
like a summer storm.

He gathered himself
on an airy shelf

in a far-off place
and there he was!

heart of fire,
hoof of daring,

and (if you believe such things)
sometimes, wings.

He stood
lean and regal,

so rare and good
that lions would fall

before him,
kindly and tame.

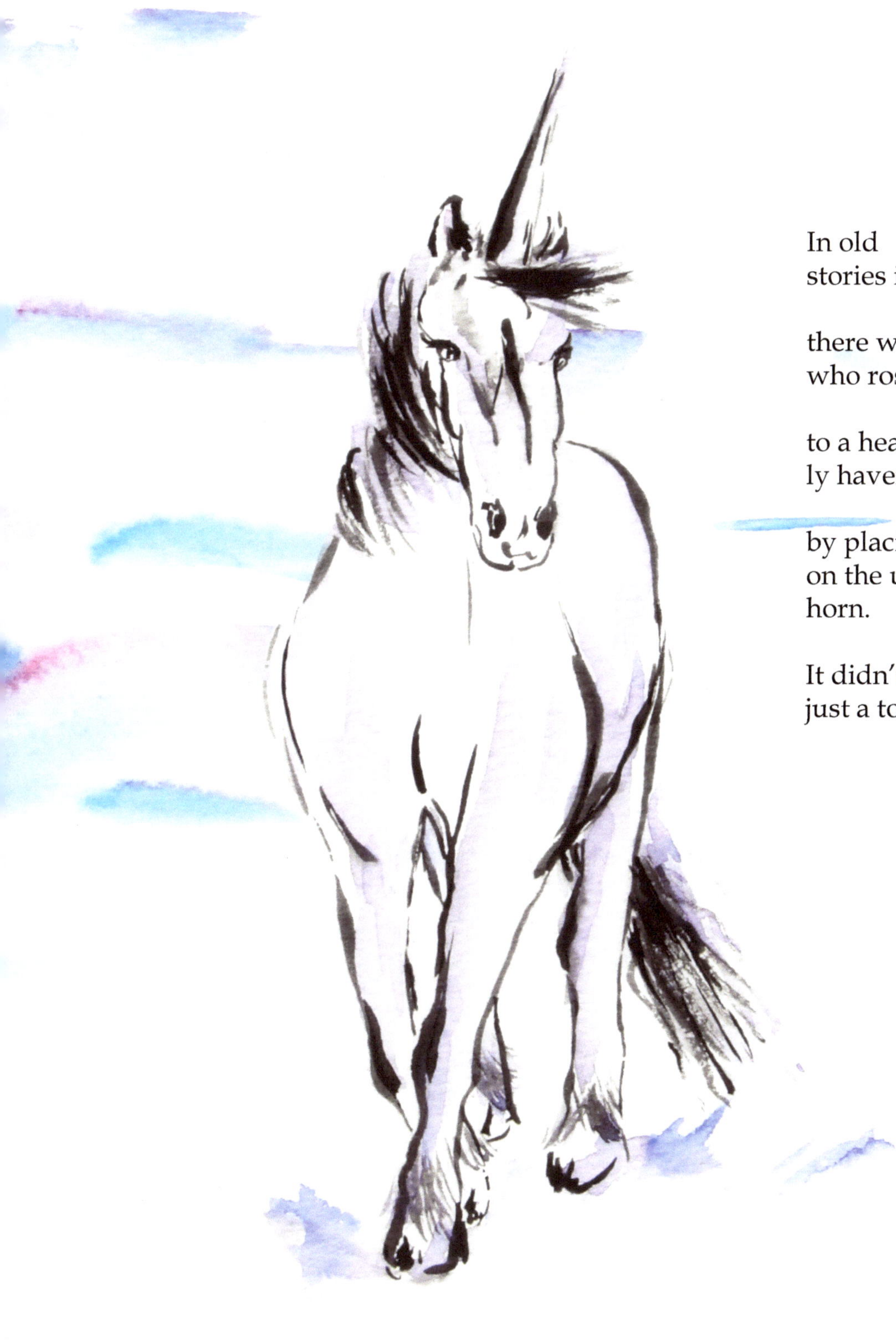

In old
stories it's told

there were those
who rose

to a heaven-
ly haven

by placing a hand
on the unicorn's
horn.

It didn't take much—
just a touch.

OWL

The owl
mostly
makes ghostly
notes
from her nighttime
perch.
For hours
at a stretch
she marks
the dark
with her lullaby
sound,
round
as her eyes,
wide open
to catch
the slightest motion
on the ground.

When
something detectable
moves
it becomes delectable,
and the stolid
old stationary
owl
slips

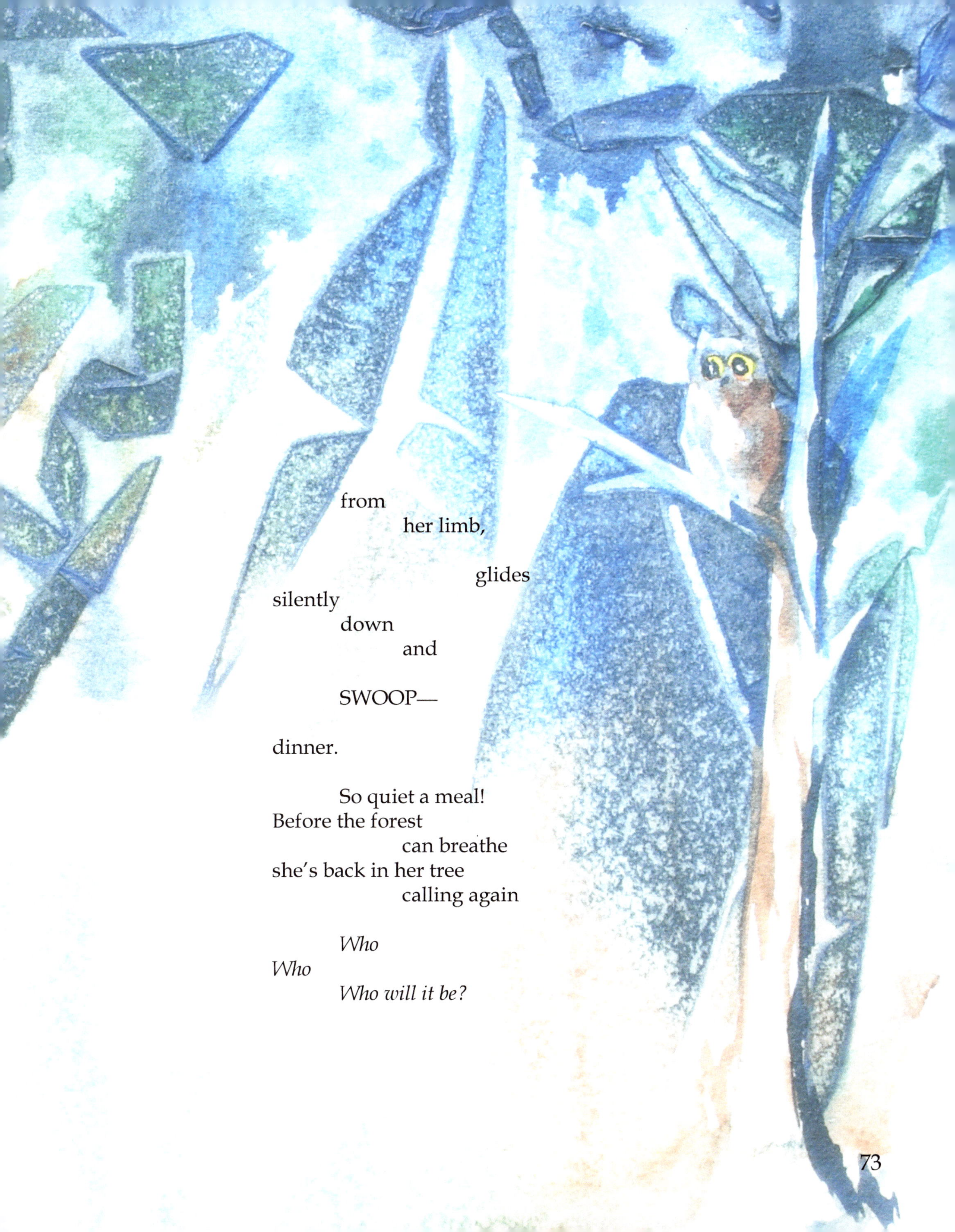

from
her limb,

glides
silently
down
and

SWOOP—

dinner.

So quiet a meal!
Before the forest
can breathe
she's back in her tree
calling again

Who
Who
Who will it be?

WOLF

He is the dark shape
slipping among the lodgepole pines,
leaving his tracks in the snow.
Flakes from the low branches
brush his coat, glistening silver
in the early morning light.
He's there for a few moments,
almost haunting the woods,
keeping himself moving in the cold.
As the sun rises his shadow
seems to sharpen against the snow.
Then he's no longer there,
gone on to another place.
Snow begins to fall again.
In an hour or so it will cover his tracks,
as if he had never been
a dark shape slipping among the pines.

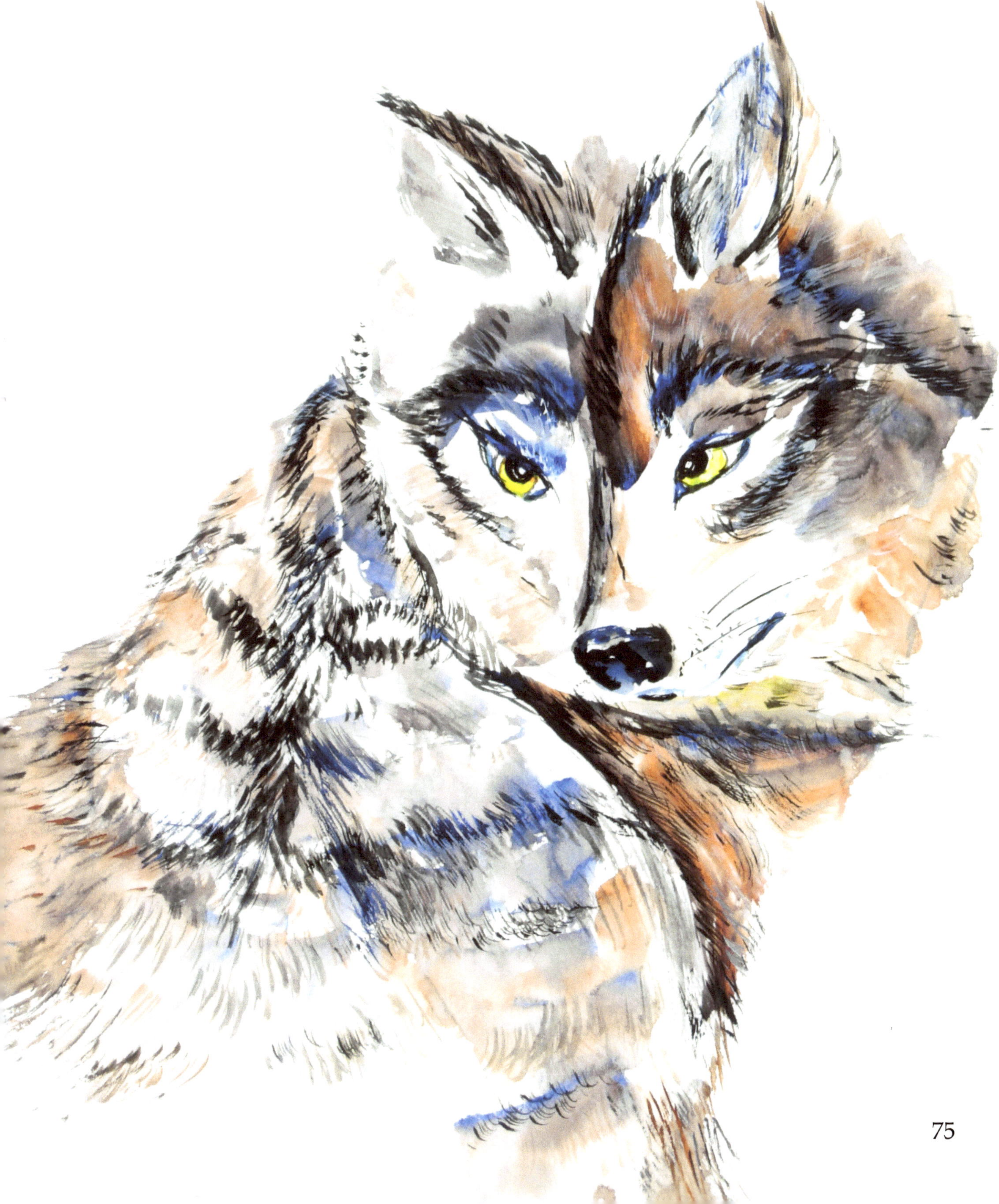

KOALA AND KIWI

Koala bear sat in his tree.
He called down to the brown kiwi,
"Come on up and play with me."

Kiwi grunted from his lair,
"I have no wings to fly up there.
Why don't you come and grub down here?"

Koala pondered that a bit.
"It's awful dark down in your pit.
There'd be no place for me to sit."

"I'm not a percher, sad to say,"
Kiwi snorted, "and there's no way
I'd dare approach the light of day."

Koala chewed his leaf a tad
and scratched his ear. And then re-chewed.
"That we can't get together's sad."

"Well, maybe," Kiwi said, "but see
how perfect this bush floor can be
for a pear-shaped, shaggy lump like me.

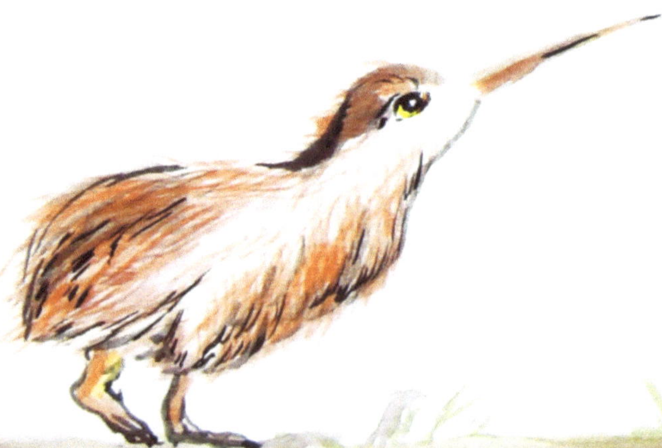

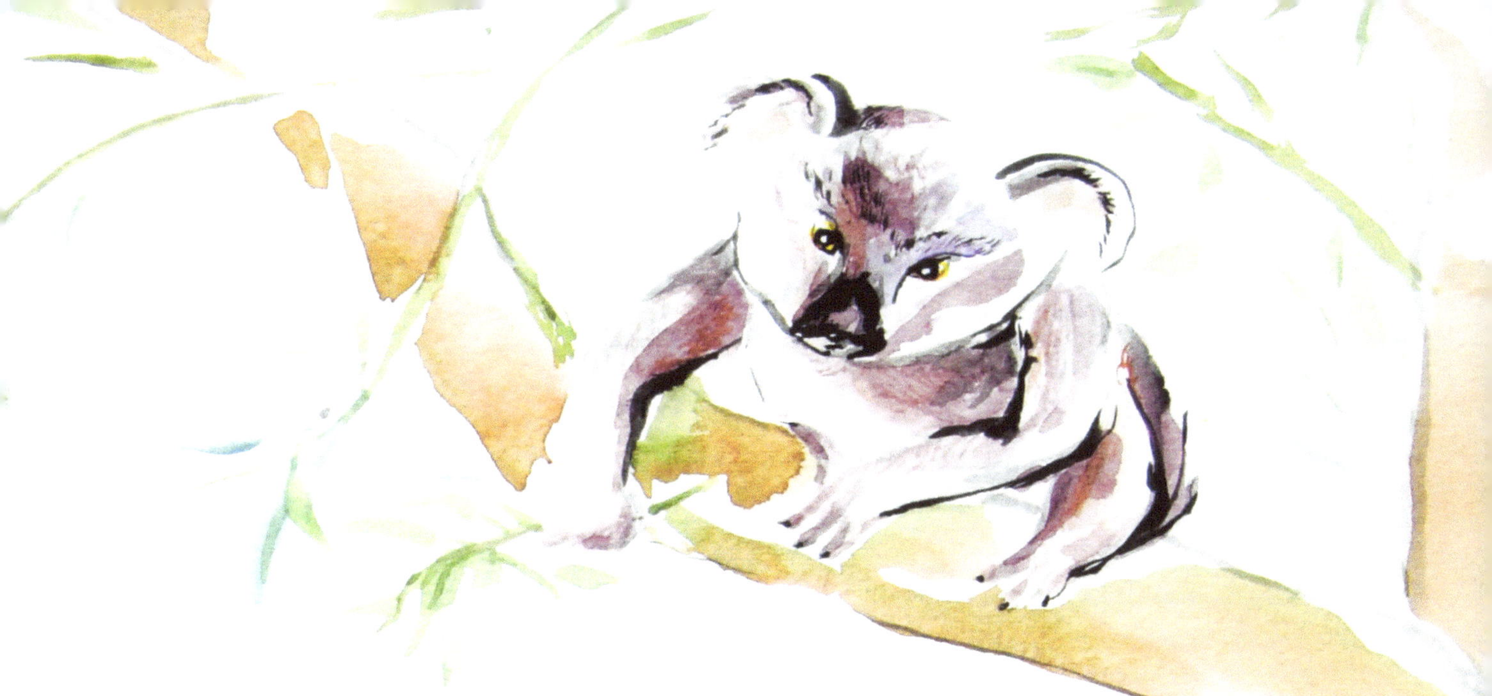

I'd be an alien in a tree."
The whole thing was a mystery,
Koala thought, that two such free

and easy chaps should be apart
because each lacked the other's art.
"Old Nature has a puzzling heart,"

Kiwi observed, as if he'd read
Koala's mind. "Yet I am fed
so well down here, and make my bed

so comfortably, I'd be unwise
to set my longing for the skies."
Koala shifted, shut his eyes,

rubbed his hind leg against the bark,
mumbled and nodded off. The dark
spread everywhere, and Kiwi's park

became the groundling's shy delight.
He grubbed and prodded there all night,
nourished by his inner light.

EX-FILES

When a creature becomes extinct,
what happens to it, do you think?

What's it like to be an ex-
tyrannosaurus rex,

or a former
all-conquering raptor,

or a mammoth, once admired
by everyone, but now retired?

Imagine a mastodon
occupying her non-afternoon

or without a future the last hagfish
making a wish.

What does the pterodactyl do,
not even available to the zoo?

And the ammonites—there were so many,
it's hard to believe there aren't any.
There isn't even one on a penny.

And thousands more such enterprises—
what became of their shapes and sizes?

HOOFERS

We all know worms
squirm

and ants
advance,

but have you seen
a turkey
do the hokey-pokey,

or the garter snake
shake and bake?

WOW!

A cow, though,
is slow

and you can’t say a possum
is lissome.

Almost the most
snappy
hoofer
in the whole animal world

is a happy
grandpappy!

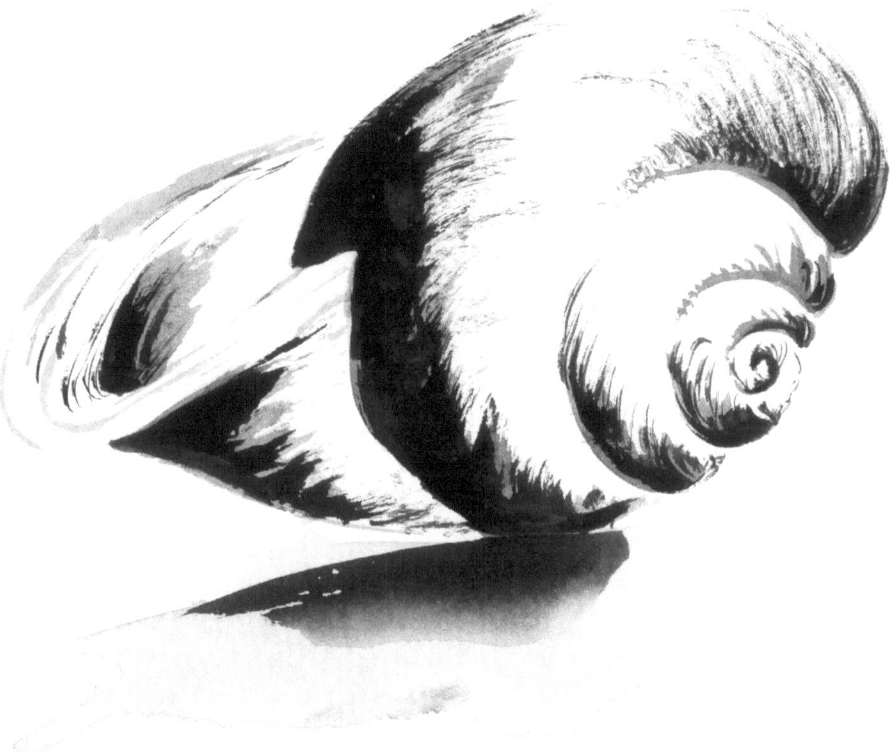

SNAIL

Isn't it queer
the way a snail
slips out of jail
when no one's near?

...OPEN THE GATES

...and the sun
        said, "I'm tired
and almost gone from my giving,"
        and went down through the gates

and rested until it was time
        to open the gates
again and rise into the light
        it brings by rising.

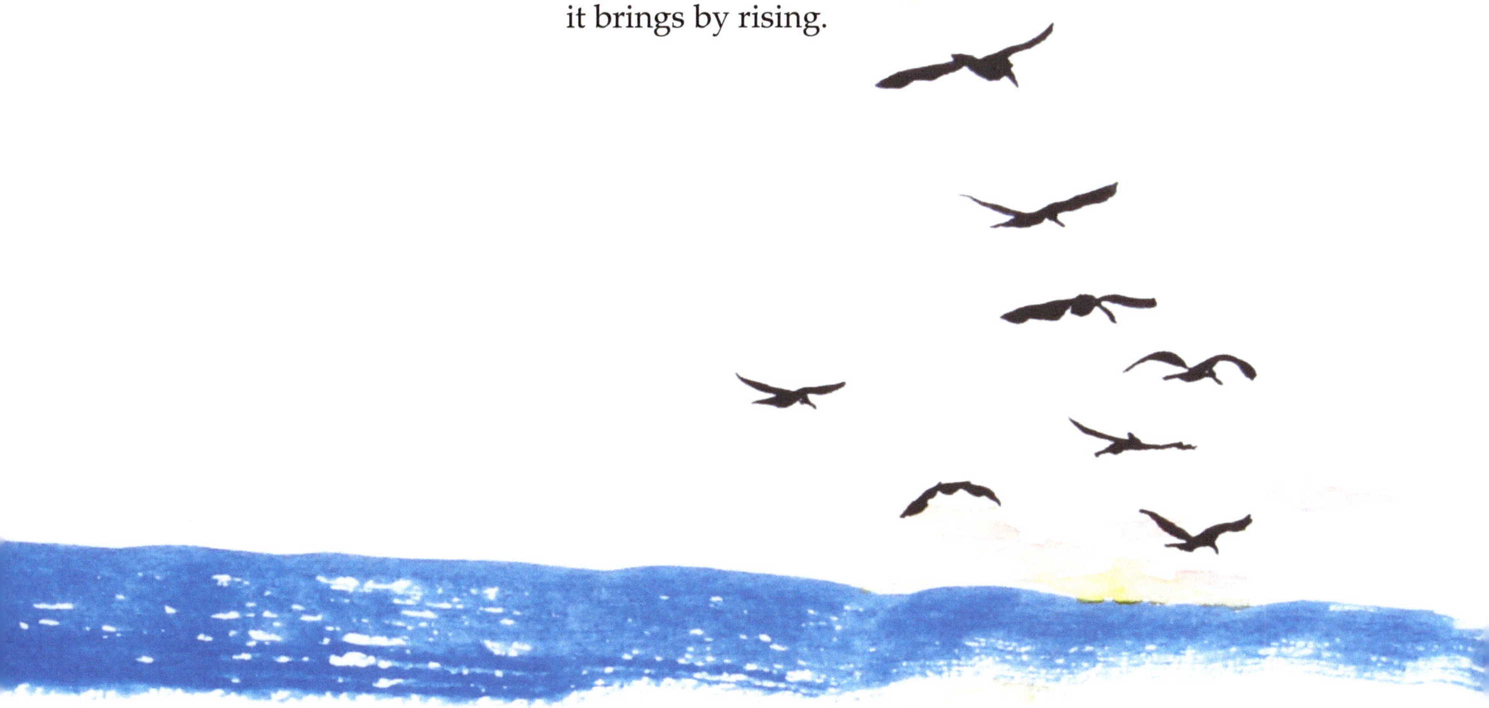

www.ingramcontent.com/pod-product-compliance
Lightning Source LLC
LaVergne TN
LVHW071132190826
846010LV00028B/105

* 9 7 8 0 9 8 2 1 5 6 1 6 2 *